Against Atheism

Against Atheism

*Why Dawkins, Hitchens,
and Harris Are Fundamentally Wrong*

Ian S. Markham

A John Wiley & Sons, Ltd., Publication

This edition first published 2010
© 2010 Ian S. Markham

Blackwell Publishing was acquired by John Wiley & Sons in February 2007. Blackwell's publishing program has been merged with Wiley's global Scientific, Technical, and Medical business to form Wiley-Blackwell.

Registered Office
John Wiley & Sons Ltd, The Atrium, Southern Gate, Chichester, West Sussex, PO19 8SQ, United Kingdom

Editorial Offices
350 Main Street, Malden, MA 02148-5020, USA
9600 Garsington Road, Oxford, OX4 2DQ, UK
The Atrium, Southern Gate, Chichester, West Sussex, PO19 8SQ, UK

For details of our global editorial offices, for customer services, and for information about how to apply for permission to reuse the copyright material in this book please see our website at www.wiley.com/wiley-blackwell.

The right of Ian S. Markham to be identified as the author of this work has been asserted in accordance with the Copyright, Designs and Patents Act 1988.

Library of Congress Cataloging-in-Publication Data
Markham, Ian S.
  Against Atheism : why Dawkins, Hitchens, and Harris are fundamentally wrong / Ian S. Markham.
    p. cm.
  Includes bibliographical references and index.
  ISBN 978-1-4051-8964-4 (hardcover : alk. paper) – ISBN 978-1-4051-8963-7 (pbk. : alk. paper)
  1. Dawkins, Richard, 1941- God delusion. 2. Hitchens, Christopher. God is not great. 3. Harris, Sam, 1967- End of faith. 4. Apologetics. 5. Atheism. I. Title.

BL2775.3.D393M36 2010
239'.7–dc22

2009025994

A catalogue record for this book is available from the British Library.

Set in 10/12.5pt Meridien by Graphicraft Limited, Hong Kong
Printed in Singapore by Markono Print Media Pte Ltd

01 2010

For my brothers
Anthony and Michael

Contents

Acknowledgments

I am grateful to Richard Dawkins, Sam Harris, and Christopher Hitchens for writing the three books that have stimulated so much debate. They have all done the Church a big favor. After years of being on the defensive, we are back into the business of apologetics. It is good to see the range of responses to this trio of atheists. Two themes dominate this reply: the first is that we need to recognize there is a case for atheism that needs a response from Christians; and the second is that science is now one of the best reasons for faith.

The genesis of this book started with a delightful lunch with Sam Lloyd, the Dean of Washington National Cathedral. I am grateful for his encouragement and thoughtfulness throughout this project. My colleagues at Virginia Theological Seminary have helped in countless ways: I am deeply grateful to Dr. Timothy Sedgwick – the Associate Dean for Academic Affairs, to Katie Lasseron – the Assistant to the Dean and Director for Institutional Effectiveness and Planning, to Rev. Dr. Roger Ferlo – the Associate Dean and Director of the Institute for Christian Formation and Leadership, and to Ms. Heather Zdancewicz – the Vice President for Administration and Finance. They do so much to keep the VTS operation going such that it is possible for me to write. Dr. Amy Dyer works tirelessly as the Associate Dean of Students and also read the manuscript with close attention to the detail; Amy improved both my style and my arguments.

Rev. Dr. Barney Hawkins not only serves the Seminary in vitally important ways but has become a much-valued conversation partner. I am very conscious of my intellectual debt to Barney in these pages. And my Old Testament colleague – Stephen Cook – spent several hours in conversation with me as the project was developing. For his expertise and the clarity of his mind, I am deeply grateful. As the project was coming to an end, a small group gathered to read the manuscript. Kim Seldman, David Gortner, Jennifer and Scott Andrews-Weckerly read the manuscript with care and made a variety of important suggestions.

Once again I have had the honor of working with Rebecca Harkin from Wiley-Blackwell. Her interest and commitment to this project are much appreciated. She is exceptional in so many ways. There is no doubt that the quality of religious publishing in the world has been significantly enhanced by her wisdom and insight. The professionalism of her team at Wiley-Blackwell is outstanding. In particular I want to thank Helen Gray for her hard work at the copy-editing stage. The manuscript was significantly improved thanks to her labors.

When it comes to questions about faith, my favorite conversation partners are my two brothers. My older brother, Anthony Markham, was at Oxford University at the height of the logical positivists, while my younger brother, Michael Markham, has scientific and mathematical instincts. In numerous ways my worldview has been shaped in conversation with them both. I hope they like this book: and I am delighted to dedicate this book to them.

Last, but definitely not least, I want to thank my wife and son. Inevitably, the work of writing makes one a little less present (both literally as one disappears away to finish a chapter, but also mentally as one finds oneself preoccupied with a particular set of questions). Lesley and Luke are both precious gifts in my life that make all the difference. I love them both so much.

Source acknowledgments

The author and publisher gratefully acknowledge the permission granted to reproduce the copyright material in this book:

Richard Dawkins, *The God Delusion* (London: Transworld Publishers Bantam Press, 2006, p.319f.). Reprinted by permission of The Random House Group Ltd.;

Christopher Hitchens, *God is Not Great: How Religion Poisons Everything* (New York and Boston: Twelve Hachette Book Group, 2007) © 2007 by Christopher Hitchens. By permission of Grand Central Publishing;

Keith Ward, *Divine Action* (London: Collins Flame, 1990, p. 83): © 1990 Keith Ward. Reprinted by permission of HarperCollins Publishers Ltd.;

Sam Harris, *The End of Faith: Religion, Terror and the Future of Reason* (New York and London: W. W. Norton, 2004): Reprinted by permission of W. W. Norton;

George Steiner, *Real Presences* (Chicago: University of Chicago Press, 1989): Reprinted by permission of the publishers, the University of Chicago Press; and Faber and Faber Ltd.;

Friedrich Nietzsche, *Die fröhliche Wissenschaft*, translated as *The Joyful Wisdom*, Thomas Common, 1910, later translated as *The Gay Science*.

Introduction

Meeting Fred and Natalie

To begin this exploration of atheism, let us start with an imaginative exercise, where we attempt to get inside the mind of Fred. Fred is an energetic atheist, completely persuaded by the writings of Dawkins et al. We will then explore the worldview of Natalie, an intelligent, thoughtful believer.

The Perspective from Fred

Fred has never really believed in God. As a child, his parents, who were nominal Roman Catholics, forced him to go to church and take his first Communion. But even at the age of seven, it just didn't make sense. The similarities between God and Santa Claus were overwhelming. He stopped believing in Santa Claus when he was six (his older brother told him that Santa Claus was a lie made up by grown-ups). As Fred looks back, he is appalled that adults contrive to force this myth on children. The moment that the myth was exposed, Fred felt liberated. No longer would he have to listen to the implied threats around presents and behavior; no longer would he have to try and work out how Santa Claus got into his house, even though there wasn't a chimney; no longer would he have to worry about how one person can visit every child on Planet Earth in one night, let alone worry about those who didn't celebrate Christmas.

And God, for Fred, has all the same problems. What exactly should he be imagining? Is it a big invisible person who can read every mind and is all powerful? This person has no location and, according to traditional Christian theology, no time. So, if God is placeless and timeless, then how can God do anything? Surely, considers Fred, all activity requires time – after all, there must be a moment before the action, during the action, and after the action. Timeless actions do not make sense. And if God is all loving and all powerful, then surely God could have done something about the earthquake that took thousands of lives. Given God's abilities, this is pretty disappointing behavior.

Like Santa Claus, there is also very little evidence of God's existence. Save for the adults that persist in lying to children, Santa Claus is never seen or heard. Just like Santa, God is invisible. Naturally, muses Fred, in a pre-modern and pre-scientific age, God made some sense. There were these mysteries to solve – how exactly do planets stay in their orbits around the sun? What is the cause of the weather? Why do some people fall ill and others live to old age? Why are some nations powerful and others less so? God was the catch-all explanation. But we now know that there are explanations for all these things. We know that Newton discovered the significance of gravity in the universe to explain the planetary positions; we know that Darwin explained why and how everything fits together; we know that political historians explain the rise and fall of nations. The God explanation had been slowly and firmly pushed out.

And again, much like Santa Claus, the associated industry that keeps God alive is pretty distasteful. Santa Claus serves the needs of the greeting card and retail industry; religion serves the needs of countless intolerant, bigoted individuals and programs. It is amazing how unpleasant religious people can be. Fred's own childhood had included the customary rants against contraception, feminism, and homosexuality. Although Fred can concede that the problems between religious groups in the Middle East or Northern Ireland include many factors (well beyond the religious), it is still remarkable how unconstructive the role of religion is. Religion, as far as he could tell, doesn't seem to make people nicer.

It is odd, ponders Fred, that for centuries the world worried that without religion there would be a breakdown in ethics. In fact, all the major advances in ethics have come since the Western Enlightenment. Toleration, for example, is not really found until John Locke has the bright idea that a Baptist and an Anglican could coexist within the same country. Or feminism (he was proud of his mother's achievements as a CEO of a major company), which was hardly encouraged by the Church. Or his gay friend, who came so close to suicide due to his religious upbringing, and who needed secular science to reassure him that he is not committing a sin because of who he is. In fact, Fred finds himself concluding, one is much more likely to be ethical if one is an atheist.

Fred describes himself as a secular humanist. He isn't afraid of death: death is all around us and comes to everyone. He likes the thought of nothing as opposed to a hell or even angelic choirs (listening to choirs for eternity would be dreadful). When death comes that is the end. For Fred, this makes the here and now much more important: there is no celestial hope to compensate for problems on Earth. As a result, he has become very active in Greenpeace. As he put it to his best friend: "we have one world and we need to take good care of it."

When Fred read Richard Dawkins's book, he found it comforting. Being an atheist in America is difficult: and here was a powerful, thoughtful study, explaining why it makes sense. Christopher Hitchens made him smile. With humor and wit, Hitchens exposed the damaging nature of religion. And Fred thought the start of Sam Harris's book was brilliant. Harris starts his book with a Muslim suicide bomber. The act of strapping munitions around one's body so one can walk on to a bus and kill lots of people is a decisive reason for atheism. As a result of reading these books, Fred was moved: no longer a "live and let live" atheist (just try and get along with your deluded religious friends), he now feels morally obligated to do what he can to persuade his friends of the value of atheism. "Atheists need to stand up and be counted," he explained to his mother.

The Perspective from Natalie

"Why should a blind person believe in colors?" Natalie asks herself. After all, they can never have any experience of colors; other people who insist that the world is full of color can't agree amongst themselves what these colors are like and argue over particular experiences of color (some saying it is red; others insisting it is orange). It is difficult to believe in colors unless you have the gift of sight.

Natalie has always had the gift of faith. She was born into a family of believers. The daily discipline of prayer at the start and end of days (and gratitude to God for every meal) had stood her in good stead. "You need to cultivate your spiritual sense," she explained to her skeptical friends, "It is a bit like appreciating poetry or great music." This was her favorite analogy: she remembers those moments when opera was nothing more than large women singing loudly and how the appreciation gradually grew. Faith is the cultivation of the spiritual sense (like appreciation of opera is the cultivation of the sense of hearing) that enables you to see the divine all around.

So, in the morning as the sunlight sneaks in around the curtain or when she is sitting with her son enjoying his playful patter, she senses the presence of God. In the same way that one senses the presence of others on another table in a relatively empty restaurant, so she senses God – constantly there at the edge of her experience of everything. She doesn't doubt God because that would mean doubting everything.

Granted God is complicated, she thinks to herself. After all, God is the Creator of the entire universe: so we are going to have to stretch our words to talk about God. God enables and sustains everything that is: so God must be absolutely everywhere. One of her favorite memories of feeling particularly close to God is a time she was in church. She remembers joining her arms together to form a big circle. "What are you doing?" her father whispered. "I am giving God a hug," she replied. It made perfect sense: God is the presence that enables her to breathe, smile, love, and laugh. God is also in the midst of her pains (and she has had many moments of pain) and in her tragedy.

Her primary reason for believing was her all-pervading experience of God. However, she had plenty of other reasons for her faith. As a physicist she had followed the debates amongst cosmologists very closely. When Brandon Carter coined the expression "anthropic principle," she thought he had a point. She considers it remarkable that of the thirty or so variables that shaped the universe all of them worked together, thereby enabling life to emerge. She found it funny that the skeptical alternative hypothesis was the "multiverse" theory, which claims that there are thousands of vast universes, most of which do not produce life, but that our universe is the one that does. "It is just like claiming that an elegant garden is not a result of intention, but a vast accident made possible by a million gardens existing most of which are disorderly," she pointed out. "Surely," she went on, "the simpler hypothesis is an agent of purpose and intention, which wanted to have a relationship of love with sophisticated creatures."

For Natalie, there were lots of arguments pointing to faith. None of these arguments on their own are decisive, but together they can persuade someone to start the process of cultivating their spiritual sensitivity. As a scientist, beauty always puzzled her (why is the world so beautiful?). Universal moral values only make sense if they transcend human lives; the world of music and poetry are closely linked to the spiritual sense – it wasn't surprising, Natalie muses, that the vast majority of authors and composers are people of faith.

Natalie loves church. She loves the way the liturgy of her Roman Catholic Church helps her to reflect on her life – to confess those moments when she has not been as loving as she should have been and to receive the sacrament that makes such a difference. She is perfectly well aware that her Church has not always been a force for good – sometimes, it still isn't. But it is a bit like condemning soccer because of the bad behavior of soccer players and fans – one needs to be able to distinguish between the ideal of a tradition and the ways in which followers can so distort that ideal.

Prayer is her lifeline. When she went to Indonesia to help with the victims of the tsunami (she was a volunteer with a medical team), every day became a constant practice of prayer. "The good thing about spending every week in front of a cross on which you believe that God died," she explained to her friends, "was that one saw the compassion of God in the suffering all around." She had spent six months working in that camp before returning to Boston.

When Natalie read Richard Dawkins, it made her sad. Here was the blind man insisting that the world of colors was a delusion because he had never made the effort to cultivate the capacity to see. Although not a theologian herself, she knew enough about theology to know that once inside this world the dots connect in coherent and compelling ways. But she found the brazen laziness of this atheism puzzling. An Oxford Don who doesn't feel the need to represent the positions of others fairly before taking issue with them was, she felt, committing an act of betrayal to the very traditions of academic enquiry at Oxford.

Yet she understands how Dawkins has tapped into a deep tradition of European skepticism, which many Europeans and Americans share, and feels that it is important that someone should set out to write a reply. She doesn't want to read another polemic; it should not "do unto Dawkins as he has done to us." Instead, it should locate, understand, this skepticism (perhaps even make the case with a bit more rigor) and then provide an account of faith that is compelling, readable, and informed. Yes, she thinks to herself, that is the book I would like to see written.

1

Getting inside Fundamentalist Atheism

The Gentle Atheism of Dawkins, Hitchens, and Harris

"Fundamentalist atheism" is a term that will annoy Richard Dawkins.[1] So let me be clear: fundamentalism is not meant as a term of abuse. The authors of the booklet series called *The Fundamentals*, which appeared in the United States between 1910 and 1915, were sincere, intelligent, thoughtful scholars. They articulated their commitments to the inerrancy of Scripture, a substitutionary atonement, and a literal return of Jesus to Earth with precision and thoughtfulness. And in so doing, they carved out for themselves a position that was uncompromising and committed. There is no room for ambiguity or humility or even nuance in *The Fundamentals*. They argue for their worldview deeply confident that they are entirely right.

So the description "fundamentalist atheists" should invite a parallel because of the equally clear assertion of uncompromising truth. The commitments are different – "science is incompatible with belief in God," "religion is deeply destructive,"[2] and "atheists can be moral." But the result is the same – an unambiguous assertion of a worldview in which the authors are entirely confident that they are right.

It is no coincidence that both the Christian fundamentalists of the early twentieth century and the atheist fundamentalists of the early twenty-first century do not even try to understand their opponents. None of our atheist fundamentalists have studied theology. Herein is a crucial difference with the tradition out of which this book is written. For this author, my Christian faith requires me to work as hard as I can to understand the arguments of Christian fundamentalists and atheist fundamentalists. And the tradition out of which I am writing is classical Catholicism as expressed in its Anglican form.[3]

This is an important point. In terms of method, classical Catholicism contrasts markedly with the approach of both versions of fundamentalism. The remarkable thirteenth-century Dominican Friar, Thomas Aquinas (1224–74), has a deeply generous methodology. Having trained as an Augustinian Platonist, he then spent much of his life exploring the world of Aristotle. He read Muslim and Jewish thinkers with care and sought to synthesize the thought of Aristotle with his Augustinian training. The very structure of his *Summa Theologiae*[4] is a testimony to his generosity and care when presenting the arguments of his opponents. In this remarkable text, Aquinas always starts by presenting the strongest arguments he can find against the position that he holds. He then identifies the hinge argument for his position before going on to explain why this position is the correct one. And the position taken by him in the *Summa* was, for his day, controversial and pioneering. In 1270, the views of Aquinas were investigated and condemned by a papal inquiry, which was organized by the bishop of Paris.[5]

Why was Aquinas so willing to read widely and explore a tradition that wasn't his own so carefully? The answer is that Aquinas had a primary obligation to the truth. The quest for the truth is a moral absolute. If God is, then God must be the author of all truth. Aquinas saw this clearly. No text was forbidden; no viewpoint inappropriate to explore. And one follows the truth wherever it goes.

So it is this spirit of classical Catholicism that contrasts so markedly with our Christian fundamentalists and atheist fundamentalists. And it is in this spirit that this book will start with a careful, fair, and even sympathetic exploration of the arguments found in three books. The best known is *The God Delusion* by Richard Dawkins. The second is by Christopher Hitchens, *God is Not Great: How Religion Poisons Everything*;[6] and the third is by Sam Harris, *The End of Faith*.[7]

These books share one thing – they are all well written. They are compelling. My goal in this chapter is to put the cases of Dawkins, Hitchens, and Harris as accurately as I can and in fact, in certain places, to strengthen their arguments. I will engage in this exercise because it is an act of Christian duty and fidelity to be fair to those with whom you disagree. There is a moral obligation on me to make sure that when I have conversations with others I can fairly represent the position they hold, such that if Richard Dawkins was reading this book he would say "yes, you have understood what I am trying to say." There are seven arguments found across these three books. I shall now look at each in turn.

The Concept of God is Incoherent

Sam Harris admits that having a worldview free of all contradictions is difficult. We have so many beliefs that to examine them all is – on a practical level – hard to do. Yet, Harris writes, "given the demands of language and behavior, it remains true that we must strive for coherence wherever it is in doubt, because failure here is synonymous with a failure either of linguistic sense or of behavioral possibility."[8]

Harris is entirely right. Imagine for a moment a person who insisted that she has a chair that isn't a chair. Imagine further that after questioning the person, she rejects the possibility that this is a stool or an odd table that is used as a chair. Instead, she really means to affirm the two propositions "I have a chair" and "I do not have a chair" as true. What would you think? I suspect all of us would conclude that this is a nonsense use of words and impossible to accommodate in terms of lifestyle. Given chairs are intended for sitting, you cannot sit on a chair that simultaneously exists and yet doesn't exist.

Now this is an obvious contradiction. Most contradictions are more indirect. It is contradictory, for example, to believe that "our lives are entirely determined by the stars" and at the same time to believe that "all humans are entirely free." At first sight, the assertion about human freedom does not directly contradict the assertion about the truth of astrology. However, as one thinks further, the contradiction is exposed because if all lives are entirely determined by the stars then they cannot be entirely free.[9]

If God exists, then one must give a coherent account of what this God is like. We cannot believe in something that we cannot explain. Granted there might be plenty of mystery, but it cannot be all mystery. If it is all mystery, then we are agnostics (i.e., a person who believes that there is insufficient evidence to determine whether there is or there is not a God). We don't know what we are talking about.

This is quite good territory for the atheist (i.e., a person who believes that God's non-existence is highly likely). Believers are notoriously vague about precisely what they affirm. It is surprising that Dawkins only explores this problem in passing. When he defines God, he tends to think it is relatively easy. So, for example, he writes, "Instead I shall define the God Hypothesis more defensibly: *there exists a superhuman, supernatural intelligence who deliberately designed and created the universe and everything in it, including us.*"[10] However, he does feel that when it comes to the Abrahamic God, the definition needs to be modified. And at this point, he touches on the problem of coherence:

> The simple definition of the God Hypothesis with which I began has to be substantially fleshed out if it is to accommodate the Abrahamic God. He not only created the universe, he is a *personal* God dwelling within it, or perhaps outside it (whatever that might mean), possessing the unpleasantly human qualities to which I have alluded.[11]

Dawkins should have developed the bracket "whatever that might mean." Christians have had enormous problems explaining the relationship of God to the universe. Take time, for example. For Aquinas, God had to be timeless – so there is no duration in the life of God. However, if God is timeless, then how can God do anything? All actions require time. You need a moment before the action, a moment during the action, and a moment after the action. If God is timeless, then God has quite literally no time in which to act. It looks incoherent. It looks like

Christians are simultaneously affirming "a perfect changeless God" and at the same time "a God who acts and therefore changes." How can we affirm both of these assertions simultaneously?

One major question for believers is this: what exactly do we mean by God? Are we claiming that God is some sort of energy that is present in the universe? Are we claiming that God is something separate from the universe and if so what? Does God have space or live in time or not? If persons of faith cannot explain what they are affirming to exist, then atheism has won. If I invent a word, say "bloop," and cannot then explain what it means, then others are entitled to ignore me. We need an account of God; and often persons of faith are not very good at giving an account of God.

Of the three, it is Sam Harris who makes this a central issue. Harris makes much of the problem of evil: why does God allow so much evil if God is all powerful, all knowing, and all loving? This is a classic coherency problem in the philosophy of religion. If God is all powerful, then he must be able to eradicate all evil; if God is all loving, then God must wish to abolish evil; but evil exists, therefore God cannot be both all powerful and all loving. It looks like theism is self-contradictory given the reality of evil in the world. Harris says quite explicitly that in his view this is a decisive reason for unbelief. There is no acceptable way for Christians to evade the problem of evil. It is such a fundamental issue. Harris writes:

> The problem of vindicating an omnipotent and omniscient God in the face of evil (this is traditionally called the problem of theodicy) is insurmountable. Those who claim to have surmounted it, by recourse to notions of free will and other incoherencies, have merely heaped bad philosophy onto bad ethics. Surely there must come a time when we will acknowledge the obvious: theology is now little more than a branch of human ignorance. Indeed, it is ignorance with wings.[12]

As theists, we should be willing to concede that (a) we need to provide an adequate account of God, and (b) the problem of evil is a major problem for belief. There is one last point that our trinity of atheists stress. They have a problem with the theological discourse in general. Christians have a technical vocabulary. For Dawkins, theological language about the Trinity is unintelligible. Having quoted St. Gregory the Miracle Worker's views on the Trinity, he observes: "Whatever miracles may have earned St. Gregory his nickname, they were not miracles of honest lucidity."[13] Again Christians are often not helpful at this point. There are so many Christians who seem to take a perverse pride in not understanding the point of the Trinity. Once again Dawkins is on strong ground at this point.

Faith and the Lack of Reasons

What is the basis of belief in God? This is the second area of attack for our trio of atheists. Sam Harris starts his book by contrasting "reason" with "faith." Harris explains that "religious faith is simply *unjustified* belief in matters of ultimate concern – specifically in propositions that promise some mechanism by which human life can be spared the ravages of time and death."[14] It is true that the word "faith" is often used in this way. The moment in a conversation with a Christian, when the problem of evil arises, is often concluded by the Christian invoking two words, "mystery" and "faith." It often appears that we don't have reasons for what we believe is true.

Richard Dawkins is right to complain about those who insist that belief in God is justified by the fact that God's existence cannot be disproved. Dawkins quotes with approval, Bertrand Russell's parable of the teapot.

> If I were to suggest that between the Earth and Mars there is a china teapot revolving about the sun in an elliptical orbit, nobody would be able to disprove my assertion provided I were careful to add that the teapot is too small to be revealed even by our most powerful telescopes. But if I were to go on to say that, since my assertion cannot be disproved, it is intolerable presumption on the part of human reason to doubt it, I should rightly be thought to be talking nonsense. If, however, the existence of such a teapot

were affirmed in ancient books, taught as the sacred truth every
Sunday and instilled into the minds of children at school, hesitation
to believe in its existence would become a mark of eccentricity
and entitle the doubter to the attentions of the psychiatrist in
an enlightened age or of the Inquisitor in an earlier time.[15]

This is a fair point. It is clearly insufficient for the theist to ground
belief on the inability of the atheist to provide a proof for the
non-existence of God. Or, as Dawkins puts it: "That you cannot
prove God's non-existence is accepted and trivial, if only in the
sense that we can never absolutely prove the non-existence of
anything. What matters is not whether God is disprovable (he
isn't) but whether his existence is *probable*."[16]

Given this, the question then becomes: are there any good
arguments for the existence of God? Richard Dawkins identifies
eight arguments that have been offered for the existence of God
and concludes that none of them are persuasive. To anticipate
later chapters in this book, this is an area where I will want to
challenge Dawkins. However, for now, let us concede there is
no argument that will persuade every right-thinking person. And,
although perhaps he is a little too cavalier in his treatment of
the traditional proofs, Dawkins is in good company with his
conviction that these arguments are not decisive. For example,
John Hick, a Christian philosopher of religion, finishes his survey
of the arguments for faith and writes, "From this discussion, it is
evident that the writer's own conclusion concerning the theistic
proofs is negative. None of the arguments which we have examined seems qualified to compel belief in God in the mind of one
who lacks that belief."[17] John Hick also takes the view that the
arguments for atheism are in an equivalent position: they are not
decisive. However, our three atheists disagree with this. They think
there are good and decisive arguments for atheism.

Arguments for Atheism

There are differences between these three books. And it is
especially apparent at this point. Richard Dawkins has his own,

rather distinctive, argument for atheism, while Hitchens and Harris reiterate some of the more traditional ones. In my view, Dawkins's attempt at formulating an innovative argument is less successful than Hitchens's argument that God belongs to a premodern age and no longer makes sense in the twenty-first century. And Hitchens's argument is the one that our imaginative friend Fred makes central to his atheism.

So let us start with Dawkins. Dawkins summarizes his argument thus: "This book will advocate an alternative view: *any creative intelligence, of sufficient complexity to design anything comes into existence only as the end product of an extended process of gradual evolution.*"[18] He then goes on to develop the argument, which seems to involve the following. All the evidence that we have about the emergence of complexity in our universe requires a process, analogous to natural selection, because the processes of natural selection enable complexity to emerge. In other words, a process such as natural selection is essential to enable us to go from amoebas at the bottom of the pond, at the start of our pre-history on this planet, to evolved humanity with all of our complexity. The complexity is a result of natural selection. Now, given that the God hypothesis requires an entity with enormous power, enormous knowledge, and the capacity to create this huge vast universe, it is inconceivable that such a complex entity could simply exist prior to any process.

For Dawkins, the primary objection to the theistic arguments is the age-old question – who made God? Dawkins believes that anything capable of creating a universe of this complexity must be a complex entity, which requires some sort of process and explanation. Now of course Dawkins has opened up a possibility at this point: perhaps the creator of this universe is a supernatural entity that was the result of some sort of complex process.[19] The cosmologist Edward Harrison has suggested that perhaps the universe was created by intelligent beings living in another universe.[20] So we have the possibility of a universe created by aliens – or from our perspective – mini gods. Much like the fish tank, the "universe" is cleaned and organized by larger complex beings outside the fish tank, Dawkins's argument does not exclude the logical possibility of this universe being the equivalent of the fish tank and the controlling complex entity being a result of a process. So it is not a proof for atheism. However, setting this point to one side, it is also not a very good argument. The axiom that Dawkins must establish as logically necessary is that "any agent that can create must be a result of some sort of physical process." By logically necessary, I mean it is inconceivable that there could be a creating entity that did not go through a process analogous to natural selection. This, I suggest, is a difficult axiom to establish.

Although it is true that within the physical world a dog can do much more than a carrot because of its complexity, the religious claim is that God – as spirit – creates. So, although the axiom is often true within the physical world, the Christian claim is that it is not true in the transcendent realm. Dawkins needs to demonstrate either the truth of materialism (that everything must be connected to the physical) or the impossibility or unlikeliness of a transcendent spiritual realm in which different rules operate.[21] He does not do this. He simply asserts that in this realm agency depends on complexity made possible by natural selection. Now a theist can agree: in this realm this does seem to be the case. But that has nothing to do with the actual claim the theist is making.

We have already noted that Dawkins thinks a divine designer would need explanation. Now Christian theologians and philosophers have a sophisticated response to this. The God hypothesis, they insist, is an elegantly simple one. Now, at this point, Dawkins is deeply perturbed. Dawkins writes:

> A God capable of continuously monitoring and controlling the individual status of every particle in the universe *cannot* be simple. His existence is going to need a mammoth explanation in its own right. Worse (from the point of view of simplicity), other corners of God's giant consciousness are simultaneously preoccupied with the doings and emotions and prayers of every single human being – and whatever intelligent aliens there might be on other planets in this and 100 billion other galaxies.[22]

Now granted if God is a giant computer, then God must be complex. But this ignores the central claim of theism: God is not a physical entity. God is more analogous to ideas than to atoms.

Thomas Crean is helpful at this point. The cause of an object is often simpler than the object. Crean's illustration is a cathedral.[23] Cathedrals as buildings are very complex: they are made of stone; they have shape and location; they are full of pews and are shaped like a cross. The idea of the cathedral is much more simple: ideas do not have a location; they do not take up space; and they are not made of stone. Yet these simpler ideas are the reason the more complicated cathedral exists.

Dawkins might insist that ideas depend on a physical brain. This is the philosophical position known as materialism. And once again in the physical realm, ideas are located in brains; however, Dawkins needs to demonstrate that ideas cannot be located in non-physical realms. This he does not do. As it happens, the precise relationship between the brain and ideas is complicated. When I imagine the moment I celebrate the winning of the lottery, it is not identical to the electrical impulses in my brain cells. One cannot look at those brain cells and say that is "me winning the lottery." Thomas Crean is right when he writes:

> Materialism, then, is absurd. A thought cannot be a material thing, nor can it be caused by a material thing, nor can it be the property of a material thing. The only possible conclusion is that thought as such is something independent of matter, that is, something *spiritual*.[24]

Dawkins's problem is that he is no longer a biologist but a philosopher. And for his particular argument, he needs to defend materialism in such a way that he eliminates entirely a different realm with contrasting rules. He does not do this: so he does not establish the intrinsic implausibility of God.

Fortunately, for Dawkins, his co-atheists are rather more effective. And at this point, Christopher Hitchens is especially good. Hitchens goes for the more traditional argument. God is associated with a pre-scientific worldview; science has made God very unlikely. Hitchens makes the point like this:

Religion comes from the period of human prehistory where nobody . . . had the smallest idea what was going on. It comes from the bawling and fearful infancy of our species, and is a babyish attempt to meet our inescapable demand for knowledge (as well as for comfort, reassurance and other infantile needs). Today, the least educated of my children knows much more about the natural order than any of the founders of religion, and one would like to think – though the connection is not a fully demonstrable one – that this is why they seem so uninterested in sending fellow humans to hell.[25]

Laplace (1749–1827) and William Ockham (1287–1348) are the heroes for Hitchens. Laplace is the French physicist who had the temerity to explain to Napoleon that his view of the solar system had no need for the God hypothesis. And William Ockham was the one who insisted that the simplest explanation for data is normally the best. For Hitchens, put these two men together and you have the reason why faith is now out of fashion. The aspects of the world that used to be explained by the existence of God are now explained differently.

An illustration might help. Once upon a time we were puzzled about why hurricanes and tornados occurred. Why it is sometimes sunny? And why does it sometimes rain? The pre-modern picture of the universe postulated a God who was a direct causal agent of the weather. But, courtesy of Newtonian physics and modern science, this picture of the universe has been displaced with a meteorological explanation. And, of course, everyone accepts the scientific explanation for weather. God has been displaced as an explanation.

For a time, God was moved one stage back. God became the designer of the universe. However, with natural selection, God has been eliminated from this role. Hitchens is very critical of those who suggest that evolution is God's mechanism for creating the world. He writes:

To imagine that God is behind the evolutionary process, turns God into a "fumbling fool of their pretended god, and makes him out to be a tinkerer, an approximator, and a blunderer, who took eons of time to fashion a few serviceable figures and heaped up a junkyard of scrap and failure meanwhile."[26]

Given that the evolutionary hypothesis makes such compelling sense of the data (which I accept entirely), it strongly suggests that God does not exist. It is such a long, drawn-out process; it is also very cruel. Hitchens writes:

> We must also confront the fact that evolution is, as well as smarter than we are, infinitely more callous and cruel, and also capricious. Investigation of the fossil record and the record of molecular biology shows us that approximately 98 percent of all species that have ever appeared on earth have lapsed into extinction.[27]

For Hitchens, God made some sense in a pre-scientific age and culture. But now, our understanding of the world has evolved. The God hypothesis has been made redundant. We need to move on.

For this stage of the summary of the arguments found in these three books, my view is that Hitchens's more traditional argument for atheism is stronger than Dawkins's more innovative argument for atheism. So, as the book develops, it will be with Hitchens's arguments in view.

Atheism Provides a Healthy and Well-balanced Worldview

Our three atheists do not simply want to affirm the truth of atheism, but also to celebrate the worldview it creates. They are offering a vision: one can be rational, tolerant, committed to progressive causes, and moral.

Starting then with rationality, Sam Harris makes this a major theme. Harris writes:

> It is time we recognized that the only thing that permits human beings to collaborate with one another in a truly open-ended ways is their willingness to have their beliefs modified by new facts. Only openness to evidence and arguments will secure a common world for us.[28]

For Harris, many religious people clearly distain "reason" and the consequences can be horrific. He provides two illustrations – the

Holocaust and the Inquisition. The Holocaust has its roots in the anti-Semitism of the Christian tradition: Luther's tract "Concerning the Jews and their lies" was reproduced and implemented by the Nazis. And the Inquisition was an overt religious program of torture, where communities were destroyed in the quest for the witch. Regardless of the arguments, too many religious people refuse to open their minds. Even today, creationism is a good illustration. Dawkins is right when he points out that too many Christians refuse to look at the evidence for evolution fairly. Despite the classical Catholic tradition of intellectual inquiry, it is true that plenty of Christians are prejudiced and refuse to allow their worldview to be challenged by good arguments.

When it comes to toleration, the atheists are also on strong ground. Harris documents with some detail the delights of the Inquisition – the lack of process, the absurdity of the crimes (consorting with the devil), and the imaginative torture techniques. Then Harris moves on to anti-Semitism. He writes, "Anti-Semitism is as integral to church doctrine as the flying buttress is to a Gothic cathedral, and this terrible truth has been published in Jewish blood since the first centuries of the common era."[29] Harris is right. The history of Christian anti-Jewishness is deep and widespread. Although Hitler was hardly an orthodox Christian, the tragedy of the Holocaust was assisted by the anti-Semitic environment the Church had created.

On progressive causes, all three authors feel, with some justification, that secular atheists are more likely to progress the social issues of their day. Dawkins believes that the Western worldview is more moral than its religious predecessors. On racism, just war, and sexuality, there is a much more gentle and tolerant worldview. And the opponents of such enlightenment are invariably religious. So Dawkins on homosexuality writes, "Once again, the unmistakable trade mark of the faith-based moralizer is to care passionately about what other people do (or even think) in *private*."[30] Meanwhile, the atheist secularist would happily affirm the requirement that one should "enjoy your own sex life (so long as it damages no one else) and leave others to enjoy theirs in private whatever their inclinations, which are none of your business."[31]

Let us concede that religion has often been a destructively conservative force in society. The Church has not on the whole been a major advocate of progressive causes. The Church provided an elaborate justification for patriarchy and coexisted with slavery for centuries. Our authors make much of the fact that religions can be deeply intolerant of each other. With many of the wars in the world, there is often a religious dimension to the conflict. Religion often exacerbates conflicts. And on slavery, segregation, and patriarchy, religious forces have often been the least enlightened.

On morality, there is a slight tendency for our atheist authors to be a little defensive. They resent deeply any suggestion that morality is difficult to justify on a non-religious basis. Dawkins sets out four Darwinian reasons for altruism: "First, there is the special case of genetic kinship. Second, there is reciprocation: the repayment of favours given, and the giving of favours in 'anticipation' of payback. Following on from this there is, third, the Darwinian benefit of acquiring a reputation for generosity and kindness. And fourth, if Zahavi is right, there is the particular additional benefit of conspicuous generosity as a way of busying unfakeably authentic advertising."[32] For Dawkins, there are sound Darwinian reasons for ethical behavior. He deplores the propensity to link morality with a divine cosmic lawgiver who is watching our behavior. This is not moral. True morality is when one is virtuous simply because that is the appropriate way to behave.

For all three of our atheists, the lack of belief in God is not a threat to our moral worldview. Later in this book, I will revisit this debate. For now, I am more than happy to concede that the Church has not always been on the right side of social issues. In addition, there are many good "atheists" and plenty of utterly unpleasant religious people. There is a slight tension, however, between the strongest argument for atheism and the attitude to morality. Hitchens makes much of the fact that the belief in God has its roots in a pre-modern setting, which is less and less intelligible for us with a modern worldview. However, this is also true of moral discourse: moral language has its roots in a pre-modern setting. The issue, perhaps, is less the practice of atheists and believers but the justification for the underlying discourse. But this is to move on too quickly. At this stage, we pause and recognize that there is some force in these arguments.

Indeed, there is a social vision in these books. Rather movingly, Hitchens concludes his book with a call for a renewed Enlightenment. He writes:

> Above all, we are in need of a renewed Enlightenment, which will base itself on the proposition that the proper study of mankind is man, and woman. This Enlightenment will not need to depend, like its predecessors, on the heroic breakthroughs of a few gifted and exceptionally courageous people. It is within the compass of the average person. The study of literature and poetry, both for its own sake for the eternal ethical questions with which it deals, can now easily depose the scrutiny of sacred texts that have been found to corrupt and confected. The pursuit of unfettered scientific inquiry, and the availability of new findings to masses of people by easy electronic means, will revolutionize our concepts of research and development. Very importantly, the divorce between the sexual life and fear, and the sexual life and disease, and the sexual life and tyranny, can now at last be attempted, on the sole condition that we banish all religions from the discourse. And all this and more is, for the first time in our history, within the reach if not the grasp of everyone.[33]

Islam is especially misguided

Perhaps it is inevitable that after September 11, 2001, Islam would receive particular attention. All three use Islam as an illustration. Perhaps this is Sam Harris's major theme. He starts the book by imagining a suicide bomber, strapping on the bomb, and calculating the best moment to cause the optimum mayhem. Sam Harris writes:

> We are at war with Islam. . . . It is not merely that we are at war with an otherwise peaceful religion that has been "hijacked" by extremists. We are at war with precisely the vision of life that is prescribed to all Muslims in the Koran, and further elaborated in the literature of the hadith, which recounts the sayings and actions of the Prophet. A future in which Islam and the West do

not stand on the brink of mutual annihilation is a future in which most Muslims have learned to ignore most of their canon, just as most Christians have learned to do. Such a transformation is by no means guaranteed to occur, however, given the tenets of Islam.[34]

Everyone can agree (including my Muslim friends) that there are groups of Muslims who pose a significant challenge to Israel and the West. It is true that the September 11 attack and the July 7 bombings (in London) were committed by Muslims. However, Harris and Hitchen (in particular) are guilty of the sin of "excessive generalization." Later in this book we shall look at Islam in more detail. Suffice to say, on this question our atheist trio is not on the side of the progressive social cause. They are feeding Islamaphobia; this is not helpful and reflects the particular time in which we live.

Christianity and Judaism are problematic

To be fair to our atheists, while Islam receives particular attention, they do not spare Christianity and Judaism. Hitchens and Dawkins provide a brief summary of the contemporary scholarly attitudes to certain issues and conclude that the Bible is ethically damaging and historically unreliable. So Dawkins, for example, writes: "The God of the Old Testament is arguably the most unpleasant character in all fiction: jealous and proud of it; a petty, unjust, unforgiving control-freak; a vindictive, bloodthirsty ethnic cleanser; a misogynistic, homophobic, racist, infanticidal, genocidal, filicidal, pestilential, megalomaniacal, sadomasochistic, capriciously malevolent bully."[35]

Both Richard Dawkins and Christopher Hitchens provide the reader with a brief introduction to some contemporary scholarship on the Bible. And some of the points made are entirely valid: biblical inerrancy (i.e., the Bible is completely historically and scientifically accurate) is impossible to sustain; the Virgin Birth narratives have a range of interests at work, which therefore question the historicity; and the construction of the canon is complicated.

This section of their argument is one that can be treated primarily as a challenge. In what sense does Scripture have authority, given the way it was constructed and some of its content? This is a question that will be taken up later in this book.

Bringing up children in a faith is an act of child abuse

Richard Dawkins writes:

> Faith is an evil precisely because it requires no justification and brooks no argument. Teaching children that unquestioned faith is a virtue primes them – given certain other ingredients that are not hard to come by – to grow up into potentially lethal weapons for future jihads or crusades. . . . Faith can be very very dangerous, and deliberately to implant it into the vulnerable mind of an innocent child is a grievous wrong.[36]

Christopher Hitchens asks the question: "How can we ever know how many children had their psychological and physical lives irreparably maimed by the compulsory inculcation of faith?"[37] For both of them, parents who inculcate religion into the young are guilty of a form of child abuse.

Now the argument here seems to be this. First, one should teach children to approach life rationally (i.e., look at the arguments and determine which one makes most sense of the evidence). Second, metaphysical questions are very complicated. So, writes Dawkins, "small children are too young to decide their views on the origins of the cosmos, of life and of morals."[38] So children are not in a place to think rationally about metaphysics. And, third, parents end up abusing their power when they use their authority to tell children what to believe.

To the obvious objection that atheists are inculcating their children into atheism, they would retort that "atheism" is a good place to start. Dawkins would argue that to decide that Loch Ness is probably empty, or that UFOs are not watching us, is where everyone should start until the evidence proves otherwise. Children should be given the tools to think; and then as the child gets older they can apply these rational tools to the issues of the Loch Ness monster, aliens, and, of course, God.

While conceding that this is a legitimate argument, this is a key area of disagreement. Later in the book, I shall argue that the capacity to appreciate the God discourse depends on the cultivation of the "spiritual sense." The appreciation of the liturgy is like the appreciation of poetry or opera – one needs to be trained. And in the same way that children can absorb languages effortlessly, so they have a natural spiritual sense that can and should be cultivated.

Now this concludes the sympathetic presentation of the arguments embedded in these books. This presentation should not mislead. There are aspects of these books that display a shocking ignorance and a basic lack of willingness to research. So, for the sake of the record, I will provide one illustration. And this is Christopher Hitchens's rather odd excursus on pigs.

Hitchens on Pigs

It comes as a shock. One has just eased into Hitchens's delightful exposition of atheism and suddenly we have "a short digression on the Pig; or, why heaven hates ham." The point is to show how silly religion can be: or, as Hitchens puts it, "In microcosm, this apparently trivial fetish shows how religion and faith and superstition distort our whole picture of the world."[39]

The target here is the food forbidden by Islam and Judaism – in particular, the shared prohibition of the cloven-hoof, cud-chewing animal, known as the pig. Hitchens starts by explaining how pigs are intelligent, thoughtful animals, which are much maligned. "This fine beast," explains Hitchens, "is one of our fairly close cousins. It shares a great deal of our DNA, and there have lately been welcome transplants of skin, heart valves, and kidneys from pigs to humans."[40] Hitchens then goes on to argue that this ban has nothing to do with health, in particular the danger of "the worms of trichinosis."[41] On this point, Hitchens is entirely right. However, Hitchens then develops his own original explanation for this – what he believes to be – irrational practice. He writes:

The simultaneous attraction and repulsion derived from an anthropomorphic root: the look of the pig, and the taste of the pig, and the dying yells of the pig, and the evident intelligence of the pig, were too uncomfortably reminiscent of the human. Porcophobia – and porcophilia – thus probably originates in a night-time of human sacrifice and even cannibalism at which the "holy" texts often do more than hint.[42]

So the ban arises because of the similarities between humans and pigs; and as a result of the ban, Hitchens argues, Muslims continue to behave badly (some European Muslims apparently want "Three Little Pigs" banned), while Christians in Spain used to check on the authenticity of Jewish conversions by offering charcuterie (pieces of pork). All of this cruelty, argues Hitchens, is grounded in the divine's hatred of the pig.

The irony of this rant is that it is the complete opposite of the truth. With the exception of the observation that the food laws are not health related, this is a deeply misguided critique. Instead, the truth about food laws is that two themes emerge: the first is an eco-friendly affirmation of life; and the second is holiness and separateness from the nations.

Instead of striving for "originality," Hitchens should have spent some time with Jacob Milgrom's rather large commentary on Leviticus 1–16. The text, explains Milgrom, assumes that some humans will eat animals, but that the Israelites will deliberately abstain from some of these animals. The permitted animals are sheep, cattle, goats, fish (several different sorts), locusts, pigeons, turtledoves, and certain birds. After an extended discussion, Milgrom explains that the rationale underpinning this selection is as follows:

Its purpose is to teach the Israelite reverence for life by (1) reducing his choice of flesh to a few animals; (2) limiting the slaughter of even these few permitted animals to the most humane way; and (3) prohibiting the ingestion of blood and mandating its disposal upon the altar or by burial as acknowledgment that bringing death to living things is a concession of God's grace and not a privilege of man's whim.[43]

So when Hitchens suggests that "a strong case is now made by humanists that it [the animal] should not be factory-farmed, confined, separated from its young, and forced to live in its own ordure,"[44] he comes close to describing the intent of the food laws.

To understand Leviticus, the picture we need here is this. There are many animals that humans everywhere can eat – all of which are good. However, as part of the covenant between God and the Israelites, there is an obligation to appreciate the significance of taking life and to set themselves apart from the other nations (the holiness project). Even though the other nations are allowed to eat pork, the Jew has been asked to abstain.

Now it is true that the pig is especially interesting. Milgrom does discuss the pre-Scriptural layer, which provides the context for the food laws. He writes:

> Thus it is clear from the evidence of the ancient Near East that the pig was not only universally reviled but, at the same time, revered in chthonic cults [cults linked to the underworld], which penetrated into Israel as late as the sixth century, arousing the wrath of prophet and priest alike.[45]

And it is clear that the addition of "cud-chewing" made sure that the pig was included in those animals that cannot be consumed. Given that most meat eating in this culture would be around celebration (and therefore giving thanks to God by sacrificing the animal on the altar), there was a sense that the association the pig has in other cultures made its exclusion important.

But the prohibition has nothing to do with cannibalism or with the similarity with humans. And it is also not manifestly irrational or misguided. Primarily, the prohibition is related to an appeal for the taking of animal life for human consumption to be done with care and respect.

As I have demonstrated in this chapter, there are some good arguments in Hitchens's book. And these good arguments need serious and careful attention. However, at other points, Hitchens needed to do some more reading. There are plenty of sections where this is the case and this is one such illustration.

This concludes the case for this trio of atheists. We are moving from Fred's perspective to an exploration and defense of Natalie's perspective. I hope that Fred perceives that I understand and feel the intellectual force of the arguments in favor of atheism. And I hope that Natalie feels that the intellectual tradition underpinning Western skepticism has been given a fair hearing. The time has now come to start formulating the response. We shall begin by suggesting that the implications of atheism have not really been faced by this trio of atheists. I will now show that this is a middle-class university atheism. So Dawkins, for example, is providing a very benign, quite attractive, Oxbridge atheism. If you look closely, you can see the conversations and humor of the university common room, his affection for the King James' version of the Bible, and his love of choirs. This "middle-class university atheism" will be contrasted in the next chapter with "real atheism" – the atheism of Nietzsche. Nietzshe argued that atheism had dramatic implications for how one understands morality and truth, while for Dawkins there are no implications of atheism for morality and truth. As we compare Dawkins and Nietzsche, we shall discover that Nietzsche has the better arguments. Such that at the end of chapter 2, the choice will be clarified – it is either Nietzsche's atheism or theism.

2

Nietzsche

The Last Real Atheist

It might be considered odd to start the response to the trio of atheists by introducing yet another atheist. However, atheists are not all the same. In the worldview of Dawkins, Hitchens, and Harris, God is seen as an add-on to one's worldview that one can and should easily reject. So they look at the world and see tables, chairs, trees, and animals. In addition, they recognize that there are feelings (some of which are very powerful and creative). There are also great human achievements – such as art, poetry, and music. They are deeply impressed by the capacity of the human mind to explain the complexity of the world and the remarkable achievements of science. All of this, they recognize that the theist can see as well. What they find so odd is the following. Why does the theist want to postulate a big invisible entity to explain all these experiences? Why does the theist want to add God on to the package of things that exist? This additional belief, they argue, is not needed.

Nietzsche is important because he pushes back on this worldview. For Nietzsche, it is not true that God is simply an add-on belief to other "obvious" experiences of the world that we are all able to share. Instead, God really affects everything. And if God goes (which Nietzsche thinks he should), then lots of other things go as well.

At this point, there needs to be a warning. This is probably the hardest chapter in this book. Nietzsche is neither an easy person to read nor an easy person to summarize. At the end of this chapter, there is a summary that is sufficient for understanding the rest of the argument. And, given there is much that is important beyond this chapter (so I'd rather you did not give up on the book halfway through chapter 2), the reader is at this point invited to simply move to the summary at the end.

For those who are sticking with the details of the argument, we turn now to Nietzsche. And the place to start is with the following questions. Who was Nietzsche? And what did he teach about the world?

Fredrick Nietzsche: The Life[1]

Fredrick Nietzsche (1844–1900) was the son of a Lutheran pastor. He had a strict classical education. At the age of eight, there were signs of a philosopher emerging. At twelve, his slightly obsessive streak was beginning to show: he would wake up extremely early and then work all day long into the evening. Perhaps because of this punishing schedule, he was to be haunted by illness throughout his life. At the age of twenty-four, when he was made professor of classical philology (the study of language and literature, with a focus on Greek and Latin texts) at Basel, his mind would play tricks on him: he worried about unseen forces "behind the chair." More generally, he suffered from stomach pains, vomiting, headaches, and pain in and around his eyes. All things considered, perhaps, it is not surprising that his life was relatively short. He died when he was fifty-six. And for the last ten years of his life, he was unable to construct any coherent arguments. It is as if this genius worked himself to death.

His intellectual journey had several significant resting places. When he was a young man, in his twenties, he was sympathetic to the philosophy of Schopenhauer (1788–1860). However, Schopenhauer proved insufficiently radical for Nietzsche, so he moved on. He devoured the work of Charles Darwin; he sensed the growing skepticism about God in his culture. He anticipated both naturalism (i.e., the view that asserts there is nothing beyond the natural world) and certain forms of "postmodernism" (i.e., the challenge to the belief of modernity and pre-modernity that there is an explanation for reality that we can identify as true). He left a considerable corpus of writing, and he covered a range of themes: the need to regenerate European culture; the nature of education; the implications of science for our view of ourselves; a "yes to life"; the nature of morality; the death of God – and many more.

Interpreting Nietzsche

Nietzsche is probably one of the most controversial of all philosophers. The range of interpretations of Nietzsche's work is considerable. It has, for example, been viewed with considerable suspicion because of the use made of it by Hitler and the Nazis. He was apparently Hitler's favorite philosopher. It was thanks to Walter Kaufmann that this suspicion was overcome and Nietzsche was liberated from such associations. Kaufmann turned Nietzsche into a relatively straightforward humanist existentialist (i.e., one who places considerable stress on experience) and pragmatist (one who uses the criterion of "usefulness" to evaluate assertions), who denies all metaphysics – and then confronts the ethical implications of such a denial.[2] The problem with this interpretation is that there are just too many parts of Nietzsche which are much more radical than it implies. Repeatedly, he denies the possibility of all knowledge, describing science as "an interpretation and arrangement of the world . . . and not an explanation of the world."[3] This led to the quest for the "new Nietzsche," with which I am in sympathy. From this perspective, Nietzsche's views are a radical challenge to truth and morality as traditionally understood.

His initial work operated within the accepted conventions of academic writing. For example, he delivered five very clear lectures titled "On the Future of Educational Institutions" at the University of Basel. However, fairly rapidly he moved beyond such conventions. He uses wit, irony, and hyperbole to make his point. Stylistically, he is confusing. He does not provide a neat, clear, exposition of an argument for a position. Indeed, his style creates part of the problem of interpreting Nietzsche. Because of this, along with the Hitler association already mentioned, many philosophers do not read him. What they miss, however, is that Nietzsche's style is clearly part of his message. In *Ecce Homo*, he comments explicitly on his style:

> I shall at the same time also say a general word on my art of style. To communicate a state, an inner tension of pathos through signs, including the tempo of these signs – that is the meaning of every style; and considering that the multiplicity of inner states is in my case extraordinary, there exists in my case the possibility of many styles – altogether the most manifold art of style any man has ever had at his disposal. Every style is good which actually communicates an inner state, which makes no mistake as to the signs, the tempo of the signs, the gestures – all rules of phrasing are art of gesture. My instinct is here infallible. – Good style in itself – a piece of pure folly, mere "idealism," on a par with the "beautiful in itself," the "good in itself," the "thing in itself" . . .[4]

Nietzsche here contrasts his style with "good style" (i.e., good and clear arguments). The problem with good argument is that it is pure folly: it is comparable with other equally foolish ideas like reality or goodness. The style is internalized. He talks elsewhere in *Ecce Homo* of the pain involved in writing and his capacity to intuit, even "to smell."[5] So the picture emerging here is of a man who has internalized the cultural moment forced on Europe by the Enlightenment. And, as he writes, his opaque prose is itself part of the message: knowledge is difficult; truth is fiction; and morality now must be invented.

The madman

In *The Joyful Wisdom*, Nietzsche tells the story of the "madman." The scene starts in a marketplace, where people are completing the normal chores of life. The "insane man" is trying to disrupt this normality and point out what exactly has happened culturally, namely the achievement of the Western world to make God redundant:

The Madman – Have you ever heard of the madman who on a bright morning lighted a lantern and ran to the market-place calling out unceasingly: "I seek God! I seek God!" – As there were many people standing about who did not believe in God, he caused a great deal of amusement. Why! is he lost? said one. Has he strayed away like a child? said another. Or does he keep himself hidden? Is he afraid of us? Has he taken a sea voyage? Has he emigrated? the people cried out laughingly, all in a hubbub. The insane man jumped into their midst and transfixed them with his glances. "Where is God gone?" he called out. "I mean to tell you! We have killed him, – you and I! We are all his murderers! But how have we done it? How were we able to drink up the sea? Who gave us the sponge to wipe away the whole horizon? What did we do when we loosened this earth from its sun? Whither does it now move? Whither do we move? Away from all suns? Do we not dash on unceasingly? Backwards, sideways, forwards, in all directions? Is there still an above and below? Do we not stray, as through infinite nothingness? Does not empty space breathe upon us? Has it not become colder? Does not night come on continually, darker and darker? Shall we not have to light lanterns in the morning? Do we not hear the noise of the grave diggers who are burying God? . . . God is dead! God remains dead! And we have killed him! How shall we console ourselves, the most murderous of all murderers? . . . Is not the magnitude of this deed too great for us? Shall we not ourselves have to become Gods, merely to seem worthy of it? There never was a greater event, – and on account of it, all who are born after us belong to a higher history than any history hitherto!" Here the madman was silent and looked again at his hearers; they also were silent and looked at him in surprise. At last he threw his lantern on the ground, so that it broke in pieces and was extinguished. "I came too early", he then said, "I am not yet at the right time." . . .

Nietzsche's argument can be understood in this way: with the rise of science and the social sciences, God has ceased to be a cultural option. We no longer need to appeal to the mysterious transcendent to explain the weather: a virgin does not need to be sacrificed to ensure the sun will rise again. In addition, the social sciences (sociology and anthropology) explain why we have different cultures with contrasting moral and scientific beliefs. Given that they are all different, then how can a particular culture have the metaphysical truth about the universe? In *Human, All Too Human*, Nietzsche points out that since Darwin we are now all committed to the proposition that the human mind is simply a result of nature. In this respect, Nietzsche is anticipating the work of the founding father of psychology, Sigmund Freud. The point, explains Nietzsche, is this: if the human mind is simply a result of nature, then all the thoughts in the human mind must be a result of nature, which implies that all morality, art, religion, and even the quest for truth are chance inventions of nature. We have eliminated God, yet not faced up to the implications. Everything, explains Nietzsche, has changed. Nothing can be the same. The concept of truth must change; and, of course, the character of moral discourse can never be the same.

Nietzsche is an important challenge to smug European atheism. Gary Shapiro, when commenting on Nietzsche's madman, explains:

> The smug non-believers ridicule his quest; they see theism as a quaint, discarded superstition. The madman replies: God is not simply a fictional personage who can be ignored; human culture, in murdering or sacrificing it central organizing principle, now faces the consequences. The smug atheists of the marketplace (secular European society focused on economic goods) don't see that God's murder effectively eliminates any analogous principle of meaning (such as economic progress, nationalism, or other substitutes for theism).[6]

In other words, for Nietzsche, there are two targets. The first concerns the misguided religious people who still talk about a world beyond which causes events in the material realm. But the second is that of the smug atheists who imagine that largely everything can continue as normal. Dawkins, Hitchens, and Harris are three examples of smug atheists.

So in what ways is Nietzsche unhappy with the atheism of our Dawkins, Hitchens, and Harris? The answer to this question needs to be unpacked in two areas – morality and truth.

Morality

Nietzsche understood the transcendent nature of traditional moral language. Embedded in the word "ought" is the sense of a moral fact transcending our life and world. So when I say "I really *ought* to go to my son's baseball game," I don't mean that I want to go. I mean that something is compelling me to go to the baseball game even though I would rather go to a bar and have a drink with Richard Dawkins. The *ought* has an external feel. It is as if something outside is making me behave in a certain way. Or to take another illustration: Richard Dawkins and I both think that slavery is wrong. Now we do not mean by this that we – personally – dislike slavery; we mean that universally the practice should be prohibited. The underlying character of moral language implies something external and universal. It is no coincidence that historically moral discourse emerged out of religious cultures. The great advantage of religion is that external and universal aspects of morality are explained: God explains the mysterious "ought" pressing down on our lives; and God explains the universal nature of the moral claim. As God is outside the world, God the Creator can be both external and make universal demands.

The problem that Nietzsche sees is this: if science and the social sciences have explained the world without reference to God, then it is no longer intelligible to believe in a transcendent life that determines our moral code of behavior. Morality as traditionally understood must go: we need to reinvent the meanings of the language, even the language itself, from which moral discourse is made.

Here, Nietzsche has a radical proposal. Our task now, he argues, is to create our own meaning. Nietzsche wants to offer this as both a challenge and an opportunity. He shares with other post-Enlightenment thinkers a strong antagonism to religion: he thought it pathetic that humans should spend their time groveling around worshipping this invisible ego who threatens to send to hell all those who refuse to affirm "how wonderful God is." So our cultural "moment" brings the opportunity to break the shackles of religion.

He invites us to consider the Superman – an elite superior person. He recognized that only a minority would have the strength to face up to our historical moment. The herd will still need to be led. However, this minority will recognize our obligation: this is the will to power. Power is located in our decision-making processes. The Superman is the one who can accept the truth of our situation, accepts the absurdity of it, and welcomes the ultimate emancipation and irresponsibility. This, explains Nietzsche, is joyful wisdom.

Nietzsche invites us to formulate a different sort of morality. He wants us to become "efficiently human": he thinks it important to impose our will on nature. He thinks our invented morality should include strength, power, and the control of the herd. If you want to invent a morality made up of hedonism and the indulgent satisfaction of the senses, then Nietzsche would disapprove.

Nietzsche has a clear position: moral terminology, as things stand, is dependent on religion. Religion is no longer a cultural option in the West because of the rise of the physical and social sciences. Therefore, traditional morality must go and moral words need new meanings.

Now Dawkins, Hitchens, and Harris would all resent the demands that Nietzsche is making. However, he poses two very important challenges that they need to hear. The first is this: *how do you justify moral discourse?* Nietzsche is right: words like "ought" and "right" emerge out of a religious discourse. The very meaning of the words suggests religion; so "ought" does not mean "want" – it is not how we use the word. The focus in Dawkins et al. is on the sociological reality that many religious people behave in immoral ways and many atheists behave in moral ways. This I can accept entirely. However, the problem for Dawkins is not so much the behavior, but justification. What is the meaning of moral words? On what basis can the external and universal character of morality be explained? And what would Dawkins say to the modern Nietzschean character who doesn't believe in morality?

This last question flows into the second challenge: *surely an atheist should be a rational egoist.* We shall define a rational egoist as a person who determines that all decisions about his or her actions should be made on the basis of a calculation – a calculation of what furthers one's own self-interest. Now Dawkins provides a Darwinian justification for altruism. For Dawkins, just as there is a Darwinian justification for procreation of the species, so there is a Darwinian justification for morality. His problem is some people opt for celibacy (and therefore decide to resist the Darwinian urge to procreate); is it possible, therefore, for some to resist the Darwinian propensities to altruism?

Nietzsche would say that it is both possible and appropriate. We are, ultimately, complex bundles of atoms that will face extinction when we die. The pursuit of self-interest is the rational way to behave. Now we can be a little less austere than Nietzsche: we might decide that it is in our self-interest to be nice to other complex bundles of atoms, with which we share a genetic link. We might decide to seek pleasant experiences – fine wine across the tongue; we might even decide to be philanthropic, especially if we gain esteem from this; but is it rational to lay down your life for a cause?

Now, once again, I am happy to concede that plenty of atheists have laid down their lives for good causes, but is such an action rational? More importantly, Dawkins has the problem of a person who wants a social code for moral order, but also doesn't mind violating that code for significant personal benefit. If the moral code can be violated, without detection (or at least without consequences) for some significant benefit, then why not do it? What precisely is wrong with the perfect murder? Or, more likely, if one has enormous power (as Stalin had), then why not eliminate your opponents ruthlessly and personally enjoy the resources of the state? If one can have an extramarital affair (undetected), then why worry about the breaking of a promise made in a wedding service? Why not support the moral code for the sake of social order, while searching for opportunities to enjoy the benefits of periodically violating that code?

Dawkins, Harris, and Hitchens are sentimental about moral discourse. Nietzsche provides an important challenge. Why be sentimental? Indeed, why be moral given the worldview of the atheist?

Truth

Dawkins, Harris, and Hitchens believe that atheism is true; they believe that natural selection has happened. They believe in the possibility of the human mind to describe the world accurately. They believe that some worldviews are truer than others. Nietzsche has real problems with all this.

When the madman lights a lantern and runs to the market-place, Nietzsche makes it quite clear that the catastrophic impact of the "death of God" leaves nothing untouched. The images in this passage are dramatic. The image of the entire horizon disappearing is a striking one. Every fixed point has gone. We have murdered God but we are not facing up to the implications. Those who do face up to the implications appear to be mad. The image of madness, I want to suggest, is provoked by the inability to believe in the possibility of truth.

This interpretation of Nietzsche depends on disentangling at least three meanings of the word "truth" in Nietzsche's writings. The first meaning is *the way things are for us as historical persons in a post-scientific age*. When Nietzsche writes about a changed situation, which results from our historical and scientific sensitivities, he believes this is something we must simply accept. Something we cannot avoid, or evade, or deny. The second meaning is *the way things really are*. This is a claim to absolute knowledge or to full understanding of reality or metaphysics. Nietzsche attacks, unrelentingly, this conception. This is a metaphysical truth – a realist truth – and anyone who accepts the correspondence theory of truth[7] is deluded. The third meaning is *the way we ought to be*. Here truth becomes ethical: it is a way of coping with the modern predicament.

Although Nietzsche's argument is, by definition, difficult to formulate clearly, we can summarize it thus: we live in a scientific age, which means a universe without God, where everything evolved (the first meaning). If everything evolved, then human minds and logic must have evolved too. Given this genesis for rationality itself, it is impossible that anything can be "true" in an absolute sense. We are historical people with partial perspectives who impose order on our experience (the second meaning). This awareness will free us from the shackles of metaphysics; it should be liberating; so we need to redefine truth in order to affirm life (the third meaning).

Let us look at how Nietzsche moves between these three different meanings of truth. "On Truth and Lies in a Nonmoral Sense" captures the oscillation between the first two meanings of truth. Nietzsche is preoccupied with the origins of rationality. He starts the article by musing on the way that the human capacity to know has created a certain vanity. It is difficult to illustrate, explains Nietzsche, "how miserable, how shadowy and transient, how aimless and arbitrary the human intellect looks within nature. There were eternities during which it did not exist."[8] At this stage, Nietzsche is assuming that evolutionary science is true (the first meaning). Reading on, we are offered some of the standard arguments for skepticism: all humans do is "glide over the surface of things and see 'forms.' Their senses nowhere lead to *truth*; on the contrary, they are content to receive stimuli and, as it were, to engage in a groping game on the back of things. Moreover, man permits himself to be deceived in his dreams every night of his life."[9] Nietzsche's use of the word "truth" here is clearly meant in the second sense. Truth has become unknowable. The rest of the essay is preoccupied with this unknowable truth. He is puzzled as to where the quest for truth can come from. So "the 'thing in itself' (which is precisely what the pure truth, apart from any consequences, would be) is likewise something quite incomprehensible to the creator of language and something not in the least worth striving for."[10] Language, for Nietzsche, creates the illusion of knowledge, because it imposes order on experience. But to suggest it is real knowledge is, for Nietzsche, absurd. At the heart of the essay, he provides a definition of what I am calling his second meaning:

> What then is truth? A movable host of metaphors, metonymies, and anthropomorphisms: in short, a sum of human relations which have been poetically and rhetorically intensified, transferred, and embellished, and which, after long usage, seems to a people fixed, canonical, and binding. Truths are illusions which we have forgotten are illusions; they are metaphors that have become

worn out and have been drained of sensuous force, coins which
have lost their embossing and are now considered as metal and
no longer as coins.[11]

Thus far, then, Nietzsche seems to be arguing that what we now
know is that truth is not knowable. "True" statements once had
power; now they are considered as metal and no longer coins.
To the obvious question – how can it be true that there is no
truth? – he provides no answer. He cannot.

The rest of the essay examines the social nature of language
and its implications for truth. These are further arguments for
his second meaning. Given that society invents the categories
(to take his example, we provide a definition of mammal), it is
no achievement to find an example and pronounce that we have
discovered the "truth." This is a "thoroughly anthropomorphic
truth which contains not a single point which would be 'true in
itself' or really and universally valid apart from man."[12]

Nietzsche in this essay has moved from the truth (the first meaning) of naturalism (i.e., there is no God – an evolutionary view
of life is entirely true), to the implications for truth (the second
meaning). To complain that this is manifestly self-refuting is to
miss the point. For Nietzsche, this is us. He is describing our
predicament. It is this predicament that we find in all his work.

Human, All Too Human was Nietzsche's second book. It broke
all the conventions of traditional academic study, thereby
anticipating Nietzsche's famous style. He starts this volume by
distinguishing between two types of philosophy: metaphysical
philosophy, which produces truths (the second meaning) which
are no longer believable; and historical philosophy, which produces truths whose implications encapsulate our modern dilemma
(the first meaning). The question is the same as in "On Truth
and Lies in a Nonmoral Sense": "how can something originate
in its opposite, for example rationality in irrationality, the sen-
tient in the dead, logic in unlogic, disinterested contemplation
in covetous desire, living for others in egoism, truth in error?"[13]
Metaphysical philosophy solves the problem by referring to the
transcendent: historical philosophy knows that the answer is found
in chemistry. So Nietzsche writes, "All we require, and what can

be given us only now the individual sciences have attained their present level, is a *chemistry* of the moral, religious and aesthetic conceptions and sensations . . ."[14]

Nietzsche is here assuming the truth (first meaning) of our post-Darwinian age. What occupies him now are the implications of that. He moves on to argue there is nothing that could be said to be true of every human, and slips into the second meaning of truth: "But everything has become: there are no eternal facts, just as there are no absolute truths."[15]

Another discussion of reason and rationality is found in *The Gay Science*, book two. We recognize the problem: science generates an anthropology which does not justify the realist view of truth. We are passionate, emotional animals: yet knowledge requires dispassionate detachment. A realist is a sober person who cannot admit to being drunk. So he writes:

> To the realists. – You sober people who feel well armed against passion and fantasies and would like to turn your emptiness into a matter of pride and an ornament: you call yourself realists and hint that the world really is the way it appears to you.[16]

For these realists, the problem is that "realism" is not justified by our knowledge of what we are (first meaning); we are passionate, drunk people. Both the realist and the non-realist have their origins in nature.

> There is no "reality" for us – not for you either, my sober friends. We are not nearly as different as you think, and perhaps our good will to transcend intoxication is as respectable as your faith that you are altogether incapable of intoxication.[17]

Nietzsche is here introducing a third state, which corresponds with my third "truth." We have the realists (who imagine they will never get drunk), the passionate animals (who are drunk – i.e., recognize their ontology), and Nietzsche and allies (who are trying to transcend intoxication). The passionate animals have truth number one; the realists are guilty of believing truth number two; while Nietzsche is going to advocate a new way (truth number three).

This new response is sketched out by him in section 58:

> Only as creators! – This has given me the greatest trouble and still does: to realise that what things are called is incomparably more important than what they are. . . . What at first was appearance becomes in the end, almost invariably, the essence and is effective as such. How foolish it would be to suppose that one only need to point to this origin and this misty strand of delusion in order to destroy the world that counts for real, so-called "reality." We can destroy only as creators. – But let us not forget this either: it is enough to create new names and estimations and probabilities in order to create in the long run new "things."[18]

So now language provides the way forward. Naming creates the problem; however, naming also provides the solution. For Nietzsche, it is the recognition of this power within each of us that provides the antidote to nihilism. No longer does a reality (God or even science) control us, but we can become the controllers. All we can do is interpret the signs that make up experience: once we imagined the interpretation was given; now Nietzsche believes we must give it. The Nietzschean circle is now complete: science provides a historical given (a self-understanding we must live with) – the first meaning; the historical sensitivity has made the traditional understanding of truth unintelligible – the second meaning; we must now seize the moment, say yes to life, and impose our will on the world around us – the third meaning.

A world without God is a world without logic. In *Beyond Good and Evil*, Nietzsche sets out the main arguments. Psychology will illuminate the process of knowing. The logician assumes a control by the knower over the known. But this is false. Nietzsche writes:

> As for the superstitions of the logicians, I shall never tire of underlining a concise little fact which these superstitious people are loath to admit – namely, that a thought comes when "it" wants, not when "I" want; so that it is a falsification of the facts to say: the subject "I" is the condition of the predicate "think."[19]

The answer is for logicians to relinquish their expertise over "knowing" to the psychologists. "All psychology has hitherto remained anchored to moral prejudices and timidities: it has not ventured into the depths. . . . For psychology is now once again the road to the fundamental problems.[20] Once again, we see a true science (first meaning) undermining the logic assumed by truth (second meaning). The first causes the second.

In book five of *The Gay Science*, Nietzsche tackles the issue of the origins of knowledge. Here he suggests that claims to knowledge are ways of containing the world: we domesticate the unknown and strange by calling it "known." Nietzsche writes, "Look, isn't our need for knowledge precisely this need for the familiar, the will to uncover under everything strange, unusual, and questionable something that no longer disturbs us? Is it not the instinct of fear that bids us to know? And is the jubilation of those who attain knowledge not the jubilation over the restoration of a sense of security?"[21] He is here commending an ethic that takes the risk of living with the lack of certainty that a life without truth (second meaning) will entail. He is setting the scene for *Thus Spake Zarathustra*.

Primarily, *Thus Spake Zarathustra* is the development of our third meaning of truth. R. J. Hollingdale is correct in his summary of the book, when he writes:

> To give life a meaning: that has been the grand endeavour of all who have preached "truth"; for unless life is given a meaning it has none. At this level, truth is not something that can be proved or disproved: it is something which you *determine upon*, which, in the language of the old psychology, you *will*. It is not something waiting to be discovered, something to which you submit or at which you halt: it is something you *create*, it is the expression of a particular kind of life and being which has, in you, ventured to assert itself. . . . What then ultimately is the answer to Pilate's question? It is: truth is will to power.[22]

In my view, Nietzsche builds on the first and second meanings. The Superman is the person who accepts our historical position (first meaning), is ready to grasp the implications (second meaning), and then is able to create the meaning for the way forward.

The book starts with the pronouncement by Zarathustra that God is dead. Then we have the first sermon preached to people assembled in the market square. The madness of the message is still there. Zarathustra concludes his message by saying, "Behold, I teach you the Superman: he is this lightning, he is this madness!"[23] Madness captures the radical message (a truth where truth is not possible). But the madness is cleansing: "Where is the madness, with which you should be cleansed?"[24] And it is controlled, because truth is redefined: "Behold, I teach you the Superman. The Superman is the meaning of the earth. Let your will say: The Superman shall be the meaning of the earth!"[25] Meaning is no longer discovered, but imposed. The Superman has found the answer. It is the next development in human evolutionary history: it is, in short, the only response to our historical situation.

The three meanings of truth pervade *Thus Spake Zarathustra*. The backdrop remains the current scientific situation – a world in which God is dead. Truth, in any absolute sense, remains impossible. Nietzsche actually says that the whole message might be a deception. At the end of part one, Zarathustra's disciples are instructed to go away: "Truly, I advise you: go away from me and guard yourself against Zarathustra! And better still: be ashamed of him! Perhaps he has deceived you."[26] So Nietzsche reintroduces, at the heart of his argument in this book, his absolute scepticism about truth. Yet, throughout this book, he is commending a new vision of truth: one that enables humans to take control.

In the *Twilight of Idols*, Nietzsche sets out a history behind the concept of truth. In "How the 'True World' Finally Became a Fiction," he writes:

1. The true world, attainable for the wise, the devout, the virtuous – they live in it, *they are it*.
   (Oldest form of the idea, relatively, clever, simple, convincing. Paraphrase of the assertion, "I, Plato, *am* the truth.")
2. The true world, unattainable for now, but promised to the wise, the devout, the virtuous ("to the sinner who does penance").

(Progress of the idea: it becomes more refined, more devious, more mystifying – *it becomes woman*, it becomes Christian . . .)

3. The true world, unattainable, unprovable, unpromisable, but a consolation, an obligation, an imperative, merely by virtue of being thought.

    (The old sun basically, but glimpsed through fog and skepticism; the idea become sublime, pallid, Nordic, Königsbergian.)

4. The true world – unattainable? In any case, unattained. And if it is unattained, it is also *unknown*. And hence it is not consoling, redeeming, or obligating either; to what could something unknown obligate us? . . .

    (Gray dawn. First yawnings of reason. Rooster's crow of positivism.)

5. The "true world" – an idea with no use anymore, no longer even obligating – an idea become useless, superfluous, *hence* a refuted idea: let's do away with it!

    (Bright day; breakfast; return of *bons sens* [good sense] and cheerfulness; Plato blushes; pandemonium of all free spirits.)

6. We have done away with the true world: what world is left over? The apparent one, maybe? . . . But no! *Along with the true world, we have also done away with the apparent!*

    (Midday; moment of the shortest shadow; end of the longest error; high point of humanity; INCIPIT ZARATHUSTRA.)[27]

This is the history of the second concept of truth. Initially, absolute truth was located in the Forms (Plato); then it became idealized in Christian theology. With Kant, its demise started. Kant required metaphysics as the justification for life-denying morality. Positivism was the next stage; and finally Nietzsche arrived with the complete liberation from the bondage of realist truth.

Nietzsche believes that God is required for truth. The denial of God has created the crisis of modernity. It will be objected that Nietzsche has ended up in an absurd position: you cannot argue for a position that makes argument impossible. But this is indeed Nietzsche's dilemma. He is like a person stuck in a maze, which is so complicated that all language of direction becomes completely meaningless for him.

Summary

So, for the benefit of both those who have worked through the chapter and for those who took my advice and moved to the end of the chapter, what have we learned?

Nietzsche is a resolute atheist. For Nietzsche, the "death of God" creates the context. Modernity is our situation. He takes seriously the discourse of science: for Nietzsche, science has turned us into "apes." Facing up to this has created the impossibility of discourse. Argument, logic, and truth itself have all become absurd. Nietzsche's great achievement is that he understood what theism entailed. It is not, for Nietzsche, an optional extra on life. He understood completely that God was the safeguard of much that people treat as normal. I concur entirely with Nietzsche that much is at stake once one decides that theism is false. Nietzsche moves from the truth about evolution, to the resulting anthropology, to the centrality of psychology, and concludes that therefore rationality is unreliable. In a universe that God intends, then understanding and rationality are intended; in a purposeless universe, understanding and rationality become accidents that might or might not be justified.

The challenge for Dawkins, Hitchens, and Harris is at the level of assumptions. For Nietzsche, the capacity of the human mind to explain the world is puzzling, which becomes unintelligible once God leaves. For Nietzsche, the words "ought" and "right" become meaningless, once God leaves. It is odd how our atheist trio take such little interest in these fundamental issues.

The cosy atheism of Dawkins, Hitchens, and Harris is no longer available. You cannot assume a rationality and argue that there is no foundation to that rationality. You cannot use a moral vocabulary if the meaning of the terminology cannot be explained. Either God and rationality go or God and rationality stay. Either God and morality go or God and morality stay. Either Nietzsche or theism. That is our choice.

Interlude

The Perspective from God

At the start of the book, we heard from Fred, our atheist, and Natalie, our theist. As we move into the task of constructing our response to atheism, we introduce a third vitally important character. We introduce the perspective of God. For our atheist trio (and for Fred), it is difficult to even start to construct any sort of coherent narrative about what precisely a person of faith is claiming about God and God's relations with the world, especially the world of science. This interlude is an attempt to provide that narrative.

The Perspective from God

Because God has always been, time has always been. God is spirit, whirling around in a constant dance of love. Before the universe came into being, God enjoyed the intensity of love; and time passed, unmeasured, in this loving movement between the different aspects of God – aspects which we would later name as Father, Son, and Holy Spirit.

Love has a power and momentum all its own. As countless loving human couples have learned, the urge to create is almost overwhelming. As an expression of love within the couple, life is created on which love can be bestowed. So God aspires to create a universe where love can flourish.

Being God, this universe will have to take a certain form. Love is dependent on many factors; the creatures will need the space to exercise their freedom. The presence of God cannot be overbearing; these creatures will need autonomy to learn the obligations of responsibility. A stable environment will be needed, where certain basic laws guarantee that these creatures can predict the consequences of their actions.

To develop this universe will take time – but time is no problem for God. This universe will have to include pain and hurt. This is a real problem. Given the universe is formed within the life of God, all moments of hurt and pain will be felt by God. And God knew that into such a universe God would have to take human form and demonstrate what love involves. This would be costly. But the love project is worth it.

From the perspective of eternity, the creatures that will emerge in this process will only be on a planet for a moment. But this moment should be sufficient to learn about the centrality of love – the challenge of giving and receiving love. The lessons of love are difficult to learn. The temptation to exercise freedom in damaging ways is very strong. Sin rapidly becomes a major problem: humans cannot resist exercising their freedom in deeply destructive ways.

One inevitable side-effect of this stable universe will be an environment that can be challenging at times; yet, ironically, it is in such challenging moments that these creatures will see what really matters. The centrality of love is seen when humans have the ephemeral stripped away.

For some lives, they will not learn the lessons of love. These lives will need more time in a stage beyond this universe. However, for most, perhaps ultimately all, this universe will be sufficient to prepare that life to share the life of God and enjoy love forever.

So the creatorial project took shape. The aspect of God responsible for creating takes the lead – the primordial force of the Father instigates the Big Bang. The formation of life will require a perfectly balanced universe, where all the factors are working together. Given we can see something of the nature of God through the creation, the revealing aspect of the Son is also at work. And given all of God's work at any moment is made possible by the aspect of God that makes God immediate and present, the Spirit is also at work.

It took a billion years for love to start producing the first galaxies and stars. After a further 10 billion years, stars started to die, creating that crucial ingredient "carbon" that is the basis of life. All through this process, God was using the remarkable structure of the universe (at the sub-atomic level) to progress, guide, and organize the project.

The solar system for Earth came into existence about four and a half billion years ago. A billion years after the start of the Earth, some molecules emerged that were able to replicate themselves. Genetic code had arrived: the Earth's atmosphere started to contain oxygen and photosynthesis evolved, putting in place the crucial means by which the Sun's energy can be trapped by living plants for survival.

Animal life is a relatively recent arrival on this planet; 700 million years ago, worms and jellyfish were in control. Then 350 million years ago, insects, ferns, and amphibians emerged. Mammals arrived just 200 million years ago. And 70 million years ago, the dinosaurs died out. It was in Africa that God allowed human history to start. About 7 million years ago, some of the African apes split into three populations – one evolved into gorillas, the second into chimps, and the third into humans.

God was in no hurry. All life was special and was part of the divine project of redemption (yes, including the dinosaurs). The apparent waste of evolution was special to God. The human evolutionary line was basically upright 4 million years ago and had an increase in brain size about 2.5 million years ago. God allowed different forms of humans to emerge; and it is the group emerging just 50,000 years ago whom we would recognize as family.

Humanity had arrived. Social order would be discovered. Constantly, God was present and many people sensed God's presence. In different parts of the world attempts were made by humanity to interpret God – so religion emerged. Some of these attempts were accurate; others were less so.

Without overwhelming human lives, God constantly worked within creation to disclose the demands of love. About 3,800 years ago, a particular narrative of a people became important. Abraham inspired monotheism – the witness to the unity of God and the oneness of God to the world. It was from the Jewish people that God would provide the definite disclosure of God in a life. Just 2,000 years ago, a baby was born called Jesus. The Eternal Word, the second person of the Trinity, was completely present in that child. It was out of that life, death, and resurrection that the world would see and understand who God is and what God is like.

It was this life that would show us how much love can cost. Love required the death of the Creator at the hands of the creation. Love had arrived. For all the hurt and pain of the world, for all the countless species that had emerged and died, the death of God in Christ promised redemption and hope. God knew that this world was costly: God knew that deep inside.

3

Appreciating the Faith Discourse

Sometimes I wish it were different. Being human can be so tricky. The knowing and experiencing processes vary so much from individual to individual and from culture to culture. We all find ourselves born into a particular home, with particular parents. Early on, we learn a particular language and a particular culture. The words we learn are crucial: these words shape the way we interpret the world. So in an animist culture, where the spirit world is vivid and real, a child inevitably grows up seeing the spirits in the rocks, trees, and streams. In a modern Western, secular home, one grows up naming the world using modern scientific categories – a world of things, atoms, and scientific laws.

Along with the cultural influences, we are forced to cope with our genetic and biological make-up. Some are bright, sharp, and intelligent; others are less so. Some see well and appreciate art; others are color-blind (or more strictly suffer from color vision deficiency) and confuse reds and greens. Some are strong, fast, and capable of great sporting achievements, while others are less so.

We are all different. And the place where we are born heavily shapes our outlook. One rather silly, but commonplace, reaction to this reality is to decide that all truth is impossible – to lapse into relativism or non-realism (the denial of the possibility of any version of the correspondence theory of truth, i.e., statements are true when they correspond to the way things are in the world). However, the miracle of being human is that while we all approach the knowing process from a certain vantage point, we also have the capacity to determine that some interpretations are less likely to be true and other interpretations are more likely to be true.

So it is not impossible to transcend our "conditioning" as children. Travel really does broaden the mind. To spend six months living with a family from a different culture – learning the language, appreciating the customs, understanding the worldview – can make one transcend one's original culture. Perhaps there will always be certain differences that are hard to appreciate. But the person who has done this is often able to contrast and compare two different worldviews in ways that the monocultural person cannot.

God clearly wanted the act of knowing to be rooted in the gradual processes of living in families and communities. Presumably, we could all have been telepathic, but this was not what God wanted for us. Discoveries spread slowly from place to place. Jared Diamond's masterful study, *Guns, Germs, and Steel*, describes the gradual development of human societies and the factors that shape their growth and advancement. Good ideas were borrowed rapidly (for example, the wheel or door locks); others took a long time to be adopted (the Chinese invented porcelain in the seventh century, but the Europeans only found their own version of it in the eighteenth century).[1]

Scientific ideas (to start with it was only a small number of people who realized the world was round and the Earth was moving around the Sun) and religious ideas (the discovery of monotheism) move from community to community in the same way. Knowledge is always local. And the spread of knowledge always requires another individual to appreciate and enter into the worldview of the person who has discovered the knowledge. We might wish for the truth of all things to be transmitted directly into all minds simultaneously, but this is not how it is to be human.

Instead knowledge moves and travels slowly. It is also hard work. In science, it requires careful observation and math; in music and art, it requires creativity; and in religion, it requires prayer and openness to God. It is also easy for mistakes to be made. Plenty of doctors once advocated "bloodletting" as a treatment, which almost always resulted in more harm than good. The history of architecture has countless examples of grotesque and ugly buildings being built. And in religion, there are many examples of interpretations of events that turn God into the very devil and betray the more inspired parts of these religious traditions.

Knowing, learning, and sharing are local and difficult. Knowledge requires conversation, humility, and willingness to learn. In some areas, we slowly learn to trust authorities: so Richard Dawkins is an authority on evolution and Nelson Mandela should be recognized as an authority on leadership. Such trust is essential. We cannot become an expert in every area.

Becoming an expert is difficult. Expertise in life needs to begin when we are young. It is the young who are most able to learn languages; it is the young who can pick up a musical instrument and grow to love the beautiful choral piece *panis angelicus*; and it is while young that most passions arise – the passion for soccer, dinosaurs, and botany. It is partly because knowing can take so much time that it helps when the process starts as early as possible.

The point of all this is that a sensitivity to God needs to start while young. In much the same way as the learning of language or a musical instrument is helped by the introduction to this while young, so it is true with God. In the same way that the hearing sense in the young is especially sensitive (and this really helps with languages and musical instruments) so this is true of the spiritual sense. As a child, one can see and feel the divine in ways that are much harder when older.

The spiritual sense

Normally, when we think about the human capacity to know about the world we identify five senses – sight, touch, smell, hearing, and taste. However, we also know that we have other vehicles of knowing. The knowledge that another person loves us is not dependent simply on seeing what he or she does and hearing what he or she says. It is a knowledge that transcends – we know because a totality of experience tells us that there is love in this relationship.

Now of course some people find that they do not have all five senses operating properly. Some are blind and others are deaf.

One popular image for "conversion to Christianity" is seeing after one has been blind (an image that builds on the miracles of Jesus). However, for my purposes, it is probably more helpful to think of the "awakening of the spiritual sense" to be analogous to the "learning of languages."

The capacity to "communicate" is a remarkable gift. However, it requires effort and practice. One must learn syntax and a vocabulary. The evolutionary origins of language are puzzling, provoking a lively debate in the literature. Steven Pinker and Ray Jackendoff stress the remarkable capacity of the human to learn languages for the purposes of communication (and in doing so challenge the views of Chomsky and others). Pinker writes:

> At least since the story of the Tower of Babel, everyone who has reflected on language has noted its vast communicative power and indispensable role in human life. Humans can use language to convey everything from gossip, recipes, hunting techniques, and reciprocal promises to theories of the origin of the universe and the immortality of the soul.[2]

Language, argue Pinker and Jackendoff, is an innate human capacity that enables us to communicate. It is "natural"; it is a capacity that people need to awaken and train.

In one sense the argument of this book is that Dawkins, Hitchens, and Harris are not allowing themselves to learn the language of faith – they are not cultivating the capacity to communicate with the divine. Dawkins, Hitchens, and especially Harris (his passion for the Eastern traditions illustrates this) do have an appreciation of the power of love and a sense of morality, but have a complete inability to even start to understand the sense of divine that the vast majority of humans around the world (both historically and today) enjoy.

The Spiritual Dimension of Humanity[3]

So what evidence is there of this spiritual dimension to humanity? This is datum that our scientific trio ignores: however, the datum is overwhelming. The vast majority of people (both those living today and historically) are or were deeply religious. Dawkins admits that this aspect of the religious story is puzzling – hence his hypothesis of memes. However, I wish to suggest an alternative. The fact that the majority of people are religious is evidence for the spiritual dimension of humanity.

David Hay is a helpful resource at this point. In his recent study, *Something There: The Biology of the Human Spirit*, he starts by explaining a key assumption. He writes: "I am a committed Darwinian, but . . . I am [also] a religious believer."[4] In this remarkable study he sets out the data in ways that should intrigue Dawkins because of its thoroughness and restraint.

The first step for Hay is to draw attention to the significant numbers of people who report that they have an awareness of God. In 1987, almost half of the population of Britain reported a spiritual experience: 29 percent talked about seeing God in the "patterning of events" around them; 27 percent had an awareness of the presence of God; and 25 percent had moments when prayer was answered.[5] Now the most extraordinary finding results from the same questions being asked in 2000. Dawkins would have expected a significant decline. However, as Hay writes, "I was astonished when I received the results. . . . Over those 13 years there had been an almost 60 per cent increase in the positive response rate. The figures suggest that around three quarters of the national population are now likely to admit to having had one of these experiences. The great majority of these people are of course not regular churchgoers."[6] So 55 percent see God in the patterning of events, 38 percent have an awareness of God, and 37 percent have an awareness of answered prayer.

The second step for Hay is to build on the work of his mentor, Alister Hardy. Hay summarizes the work of Hardy thus:

> Hardy expressed his conviction that all of us as members of the species *Homo sapiens* have the potential for spiritual awareness. Amongst the thousands of metaphors human beings have used to describe it we might say: a presence rolling through all things, an unnamed power, God or the gods, a power coming from the unconscious, or . . . energy drawn from the earth itself. Hardy argued

that this awareness is like a sense; it is there because it has an important function. It has indeed been "naturally selected" in the process of evolution because it helps us to survive.[7]

For Hardy, we are – to use a phrase found elsewhere – religious animals. At some point in our evolutionary history, we had experiences of the "divine" that we distinguished from everyday experiences. And indeed there is evidence for this sort of sensitivity reaching back some 60,000 years into our human evolutionary history. Now, of course, we might invoke the arguments of Karl Marx or Sigmund Freud or Emile Durkheim as an explanation for this data: the problem is that the scientific data does not support this. People who experience the divine are often middle class (rather than poor as Marx would expect); their experiences often contrast sharply with the experience of their parents (*contra* Freud); and they are often counter-cultural (*contra* Durkheim).

Religious experience divides into three types: the first is the "sense of God" that countless individuals have had at some time in their life.[8] This is often very unspectacular. It might be triggered by a beautiful sunset or by a moving piece of music. Sometimes it can be a moment of tragedy that creates the awareness. I remember when I was seventeen, a few months after my mother died, sitting in an empty church and feeling a sense of love and comfort. In all these cases, the person who has an experience like this is sure that the source is beyond the empirical world.

The second type is more dramatic. These are the experiences that are cultivated, through certain disciplines. The mystics are a good example. They are found in all the major religions. Julian of Norwich (1342–1416) in Christianity, Rumi (1207–73) in Islam, Moses ben Jacob Cordovero (1522–70) in Judaism, and Ramana Maharshi (1879–1950) in Hinduism. These people made it their life's work to connect with the divine. Both during their lifetime, but also through their writings, they have inspired countless followers by their wisdom and ethics.

The third type of religious experience is that sense of God grounded in a community. The Hebrew Bible documents the experience of God as encountered by the Jewish people. The New

Testament documents the experience of God as encountered by Jews and Gentiles within the Church. Through rituals and practices, there are experiences that a community enters into together.

Now there are two questions for our atheist trio. First, how do they interpret this widespread sense of God, which countless individuals in different cultures experience? Second, is it possible for our three atheists to start experiencing the divine for themselves?

On the first question, the English philosopher Richard Swinburne has argued convincingly that this witness to the transcendent should be trusted. Given we take so much on trust, based on the reports of other people, it is not unreasonable to extend it to this realm. For example, I have never seen Mongolia, but I trust the reports of other people that it exists. He suggests two key principles for evaluating such experiences. The first is the principle of credulity (that the experiences are often caused by the object the person claims is the cause). Or, as Richard Swinburne himself puts it, "I suggest that it is a principle of rationality that (in the absence of special considerations) if it seems (epistemically) to a subject that x is present, then probably x is present; what one seems to perceive is probably so."[9]

There is, too, the principle of testimony (that people should be trusted when they describe their experiences). Swinburne explains that this "component is the principle that (in the absence of special considerations) the experiences of others are (probably) as others report them."[10] Naturally, there are occasions when these two principles do not operate: if I am taking LSD and claim to have seen an alien, then you are right to be skeptical. But with many of these religious experiences, the people are trustworthy, discriminating, and sophisticated. We would trust their reports of almost anything else; Swinburne's point is that there is no reason why this should not extend to God.

Globally and historically, the vast majority of people have had an experience of the transcendent. This should be treated as good evidence for belief. Granted the descriptions of the transcendent do vary, but that is not a decisive reason for denying that there is nothing transcendent causing the experience.

Now we turn to the second question: how can a person start to cultivate their religious sense?

Figure 1

Cultivating a Religious Sense

Let us try two different analogies. First, we have the development of language. Every person has the capacity to learn a language but this does require training and effort. A second analogy can be found with the famous optical illusions. Figure 1 shows the picture of the young girl–old woman illusion.

On the one hand, we have a young girl with her head turned slightly to one side, dark hair, with a chin touching the black shawl, a short necklace around the neck and a big flowing white headscarf. On the other hand, we have an old lady who is almost facing us – the nose touches the black shawl and the mouth and chin are right in the middle of the shawl. The young girl's ear has now become an old lady's eye. The truth about this picture is that it is both a young girl and an old lady. And with a little bit of work, one can see both.

The problem with Richard Dawkins et al. is that they can only see one side to the picture of life; they cannot see the other side. They need to awaken the other side of their mind and start to see in everything the presence of God. Or, to return to the first analogy, they need to learn the language of faith.

One begins by allowing oneself to experience the meaning in the words "awe," "beauty," and "justice" rather more deeply. This is an initial baby-step into the worship of God. Worship starts with recognition. It starts with the awareness that the word "atoms" is an insufficient description of everything that we experience. Let us look at the areas of human life that point beyond a reductionist account of the universe.

The Moral Dimension

When we looked at Nietzsche, we noted how strange moral language is. So, to give another illustration, consider a moral assertion such as "I think I really ought to go to my son's performance at his middle school."[11] The odd word in that assertion is "ought." It quite clearly does not mean "want." I don't "want" to be in a room with countless other parents all watching their child and worrying that he or she is the one that will make a mistake. In fact, one uses the word "ought" when implying that "I would rather go to lunch at the local bar, but . . ." So the moral obligation conflicts with one's desires. And it sounds as if there is an "external" pressure being applied to me.

Dawkins and Hitchens all rant against the suggestion that atheists cannot be moral. So, as I have already made clear (and will again before this book is finished), there are plenty of "good" atheists. No, the problem for the atheist is in the area of *justification*. It is the challenge of Nietzsche.

Now it is important that moral language has this external quality, otherwise it is difficult to ensure that it is binding. If one decides that moral discourse is simply the result of culture, then it is difficult to see why it is binding. It is easy to reason thus:

in a different culture, I would have different moral values. In a Nazi culture, my morality would include anti-Semitism; in a slave-owning culture, slavery would be acceptable; and in a cannibal culture, it would be acceptable to eat people. Therefore, if I create my own moral culture, then I am free from the widely accepted moral obligations that are assumed by everyone else.

It is no coincidence that moral discourse arose in a religious culture. So, although Dawkins and Hitchens are good at deciding to affirm basic moral values, it is difficult to see how the discourse is justified. And, more importantly, Dawkins has a major problem with those who want to challenge his moral values. Now, of course, there is a danger here. Although it might be prudent to affirm religion as a basis for moral values, this is not an argument for the truth of religion. As Fred pointed out at the start of the book: just because Santa Claus is a good tool for encouraging children to behave well doesn't mean that Santa Claus exists.[12] A belief might be useful and still false.

Yet there is an argument here. Our moral instincts are very strong. When I condemn anti-Semitism, it is not simply a result of my *New York Times* reading culture; it feels absolutely wrong. The obligations to care for family, strive to do good, and build communities of hope are not simply human constructs. Perhaps moral discourse does not simply depend on religion for intelligibility, but our moral intuitions are grounded in the transcendent. We feel so strongly because we are created in the Image of God. Granted this is not a decisive argument for belief, but it should be included as a pointer – a factor on the side of belief. The question for Dawkins is how deeply does he believe in the fundamental moral axiom – "Do Good and Avoid Evil." The depth of his conviction is the first step in the recognition of the divine: it is the start of belief.

The Significance of Love

As with moral intuitions being grounded in the Image of God, so it is with love. Although love takes many different forms, there is a type of love that tends to carry transcendent significance.

For those committed to a naturalist narrative, the explanation for this type of love is reduced to either culture or biology. And, of course, it is possible that love is no more than a trick of the evolutionary process to encourage us to reproduce. We love even when there is no possibility of reproduction. However, for those of us who have had those moments when the only person in the world is the one who is loved, these reductionist accounts seem implausible.

The Christian alternative grounds the significance of love in the Trinity. We will look in more detail at the Trinity in chapter 6. However, let us anticipate one of the key arguments. Christians are partly committed to the doctrine of the Trinity because we believe God is love. If God is love, the argument goes, then there must be the possibility of lovingness in the internal life of God himself or herself (and to avoid the gender problem, many advocates of progressive writing use the phrase "Godself"). In other words, within the oneness of God there is a dynamic interrelationality that enables the love of God to have meaning.

And given that God knows, within the very life of God, the value of love, so God desires for a creation where more loving possibilities are realized. This is a key goal of creation. Now the argument is this: when we are granted the remarkable gift of love (as opposed to lust or just sex), we are discovering the reason for being.

When you have two contrasting explanations for a phenomenon, it is legitimate to ask which makes "more sense" of the phenomenon. Again, as a pointer, the suggestion I am making is that the Christian narrative makes more sense of the phenomenon than the naturalistic one.

Music and Art

With music and art, the suggestion is that it is a pointer to the transcendent. George Steiner (1929–) in his masterful essay *Real Presences* constructs the argument with considerable erudition and care. He states his thesis at the outset:

It proposes that any coherent understanding of what language is and how language performs, that any coherent account of the capacity of human speech to communicate meaning and feeling is, in the final analysis, underwritten by the assumption of God's presence. I will put forward the argument that the experience of aesthetic meaning in particular, that of literature, of the arts, of musical form, infers the necessary possibility of this "real presence".[13]

For art, literature, and music to work, they must assume the reality of God; this is partly because it is the domain of the transcendent that art, literature, and music explore. Steiner's targets in this essay are all those tendencies in modern philosophy that deny any transcendent meaning. So logical positivism was a philosophical movement that insisted the only meaningful sentences are those which can be scientifically verified (if you can't touch, taste, see, hear, smell it, then you can't talk about it). Or deconstruction, which was formulated by Jacques Derrida (1930–2004), assumed that the cultural location of the text so submerges the meaning that we can never be sure what the meaning of the text is.

Steiner's response is to stress two aspects to the aesthetic experience, the first being the depths to which a piece of music or a work of art can reach. Steiner writes, "Entering into us, the painting, the sonata, the poem brings us into reach of our own nativity of consciousness. It does so at a depth inaccessible in any other way."[14] Granted this appreciation of great art requires cultivation. He stresses the need for great texts to be introduced to the child, and for the child's imagination to be allowed to grow. This is the key to human freedom: we discover options that are a key to human identity. Steiner warns:

If the child is left empty of texts in the fullest sense of the term, he will suffer an early death of the heart and of the imagination. . . . The waking of human freedom can also occur in the presence of pictures, of music. It is, in essence, a waking through the pulse of narrative as it beats in aesthetic form.[15]

The second aspect is that the act of creating great art is made possible because we are all creations. Steiner is here drawing attention to the genius that has the capacity to create *King Lear* or paint the *Mona Lisa*. Steiner writes:

> I can only put it this way (and every true poem, piece of music or painting says it better): there is aesthetic creation because there is creation. . . . I take the aesthetic act, the conceiving and bringing into being of that which, very precisely, could not have been conceived or brought into being, to be an *imitation*, a replication on its own scale, of the inaccessible first *fiat* (the "Big Bang" of the new cosmologies, before which there cannot be, in true Augustinian fashion, any "time", is no less a construed imperative and "boundary-condition" than is the narrative of creation in religion).[16]

The point is this: the miracle of Mozart's *Don Giovanni* (the capacity to create inspirational music from nothing) is a human echo of the divine achievement of creating the cosmos out of nothing.

These two aspects mean that the underlying disposition of the artist cannot share the constraints required by contemporary philosophical movements. Steiner explains:

> I have, before, cited some of those who know best: the poets, the artists. I have found no deconstructionist among them. I have found none who can, in conscience, accept the constraints on permissible discourse prescribed by logical atomism, logical positivism, scientific proof-values or, in a far more pervasive sense, by liberal skepticism. . . . D. H. Lawrence's is a summarizing statement: "I always feel as if I stood naked for the fire of Almighty God to go through me – and it's rather an awful feeling. One has to be so terribly religious to be an artist." And there is Yeats: "No man can create as did Shakespeare, Homer, Sophocles, who does not believe with all his blood and nerve, that man's soul is immortal." And quotation could continue. Wittily, Bertrand Russell asserted that God had simply given to man far too few indices of His existence for religious faith to be plausible. Yet this observation is, metaphysically, tone deaf. It leaves out the entire sphere of the poetic, be it metaphysical or aesthetic, it leaves out music and the arts, without which human life might indeed not be viable.[17]

Great art is born of faith. Great art also witnesses to faith. The problem with the atheist Bertrand Russell is that he had lost his spiritual sense that enabled him to see the presence of God in art.

For Steiner, this is a pointer. In fact, he talks about Pascal's wager. Pascal suggested that one should gamble on the reality of God because the benefits of belief far outweigh the drawbacks. In the same way, Steiner will wager that the real presence that makes great music possible is indeed there. Steiner writes, "I am wagering, both in a Cartesian and a Pascalian vein, on the informing pressure of a real presence in the semantic markers which generate Oedipus the King or Madame Bovary; in the pigments or incisions which externalize Grüewald's Issenheim triptych or Brancusi's *Bird*; in the notes, crotchets, markings of tempo and volume which actualize Schubert's posthumous Quintet."[18] The evidence for the transcendent is all around us. We just need the eyes to see it.

For Dawkins, Hitchens, and Harris, there is a need for them to awaken their religious sensitivity – to reflect deeply on what the encounter with great music or the life-transforming sense of love is really all about. This is drawing the analogy with the cultivation of other senses. Alternatively, to return to the optical illusion, they need to see both the old woman and the young woman. They need to appreciate that the remarkable description of the world provided by science does not exclude a description of the world that is spiritual. They need to see the transcendent in the immanent.

The spiritual sense is that capacity to see in the creation the many pointers to the transcendent: the fact of being a connected person and knowing the value of love; the miracle of beauty in the creation; the belief that there are certain fundamental ways of behaving that are appropriate and other ways that are wrong; and the power of certain pieces of music to raise a soul to such an extent that one feels liberation. And perhaps, deep down, there have been moments when a person has sensed the transcendent love all around. This is the "spiritual sense" at work. This is seeing the transcendent in the immanent.

None of these things are spectacular; they are all normal. Yet they do need explanation. The theist has an explanation. This universe is intended – a loving being created a universe so that more loving opportunities might emerge. As a result of a long process of development (13 billion years), creatures have emerged on Planet Earth capable of giving and receiving love. The stable universe was always set up so that we would emerge: our sense of right and wrong is grounded in creation: and music and the beauty of the universe are intrinsic gifts.

It is possible that the order in the universe was a completely freak chance. Love might be just a trick of the evolutionary process to encourage us to reproduce. Music and morality might be just culturally conditioned, which in the process makes both dependent on human affirmation for meaning. All of this is possible.

But in a court of law, where the criterion for judgment is "reasonable probability," I want to suggest the case for belief might win. In my judgment, the evidence is overwhelming. However, there is perhaps a stronger argument for faith. And this is where we take the argument firmly into Dawkins's territory. Science is now a reason for faith. Science now provides the Christian with a framework that makes sense of a whole host of otherwise puzzling Christian doctrines. This is the territory we shall now explore. In the next chapter, we will look at the current debates among physicists around the remarkable math of this universe. In chapter 8, we will look at how modern science is helping Christians understand such mysterious doctrines as providence and how it may provide a distinctive explanation for suffering. In this world, the case for belief is even stronger. Science is a greater problem for Dawkins than it is for the Christian. This is the argument that I will make next.

4
Physics

The Grown-up Science

It is no coincidence that Richard Dawkins is a biologist. Biology is a relatively new discipline, which burst on the scene in its modern form with the remarkable achievement of Charles Darwin (1809–82) and has made extraordinary strides forward with the arrival of genetics. So often, when a new discipline emerges, with a distinctive set of tools and insights, it goes through a rather conceited phase. This was certainly true of physics. Modern physics emerged with Sir Isaac Newton (1642–1727). Although Newton was a devout Christian, he provided the mixture of calculus and classical mechanics, which enabled an entire discipline to start to plot nature using mathematical equations. It was an important idea, and it provided the basis for a worldview with remarkable explanatory power. However, within a hundred years of Newton writing *Principia Mathematica* (1687), the emerging discipline of modern physics believed that there was no need for God.

It was probably Pierre Simon Laplace (1749–1827) who was the Richard Dawkins of physics. Laplace wrote a book on astronomy, which didn't mention God. And when Napoleon asked him why God isn't mentioned, Laplace famously replied, "Sire, I had no need of that hypothesis." As we have already noted, Christopher Hitchens has Laplace as one of his heroes. However, what is less well known is Laplace's overall worldview. He was an advocate for "causal determinism." So Laplace, in *A Philosophical Essay on Probabilities*, writes:

> We ought then to regard the present state of the universe as the effect of its anterior state and as the cause of the one which is to follow. Given for one instant an intelligence which could comprehend all the forces by which nature is animated and the respective situation of the beings who compose it – an intelligence sufficiently vast to submit these data to analysis – it would embrace in the same formula the movements of the greatest bodies of the universe and those of the lightest atom; for it, nothing would be uncertain and the future, as the past, would be present to its eyes.[1]

This is known as Laplace's demon. Laplace believed that if an intelligence knew the initial configuration of atoms at the start of the universe, then that intelligence would be able to see every subsequent event in the future. The idea here can be divided into two: first, everything is caused by the immediate preceding state (or anterior state as he puts it here); and, second, in the end atoms are the cause of everything that happens. The first is known as "causal determinism"; and the second is known as "reductionism".

It is odd how powerful an influence this mechanist picture of the universe has had on our culture. It is obviously contentious. Keith Ward observes that there

> are at least seven highly dubious assumptions involved in this hypothesis. Is there nothing that really exists except elementary particles? Are all properties even of the physical universe subject to precise quantitative measurement? Can one ever exhaustively describe every feature of the universe, much less know that one has done so? Is there a finite and closed set of physical laws? Are these laws completely universal in their application, so that nothing lies outside their scope? Is every event in the physical universe completely predictable, even in principle? And do causes necessarily determine their effects, in such a way that nothing could happen except what does happen?[2]

All of these assumptions can be contested. However, let us focus on the problem of originality in this universe. According to Laplace, Shakespeare's startling creativity and Beethoven's Fifth were all anticipated by the preceding configuration of atoms in the universe. Laplace is a materialist; he, like Dawkins, is assuming that ideas are identical with brain states. This, we have already seen in chapter 2, is manifestly absurd. As Keith Ward helpfully summarized:

> In general, if there are ever any new thoughts, or any sorts of things which have never happened before in the universe, then these things are in principle unpredictable by natural science (except as a sort of guess about the future, based on how things have gone in the past). Even if we could predict Laplace's brain, we could never predict his thoughts.[3]

The vast majority of contemporary physicists reject entirely the "causal determinism" and "reductionism" of Laplace. Indeed, the direction in which physics has moved is striking. The God-option is suddenly back big-time.

The Anthropic Principle

There is no question about it: we now know that the mathematics underpinning the universe is remarkable. How precisely we interpret or explain that math is still hotly contested, but the precision of the numbers is accepted. Once upon a time all this space in the universe was a problem for faith – do we really think the Creator of it all would care about a tiny planet like Earth? Suddenly, at the end of the twentieth century, we discovered that all this space was essential to enable us to exist. Keith Ward writes:

> [T]he universe is approximately 15 billion light years in diameter. That may seem very wasteful, if it in the end only produced human beings on this small planet. Why so long before conscious life appeared? The surprising answer is that conscious life originates from carbon-based molecules, which are born out of the ashes of dying stars. It takes just about 15 billion years for stars to be born and die, and during that time the universe has been expanding from a first "Big Bang". So it turns out that the size of the universe is directly related to the existence of rational life on earth. In short, we need a universe that big to produce the conscious life of the sort we have![4]

We are living in a universe where it looks as if life was always intended.

The physicist Paul Davies sets out the data with some care. So he writes, "The existence of life as we know it depends delicately on many seemingly fortuitous features of the laws of physics and the structure of the universe."[5] So, for example, carbon-based life depends on the production of carbon. The production of carbon in stars requires "a numerical 'coincidence' to produce a nuclear resonance at just the right energy."[6] If this numerical coincidence had not occurred, then life would not have occurred.

Along with the size of the universe and the production of carbon, there is a whole range of variables that needed to be just right for life to emerge. So, to take another illustration, the forces of expansion and gravity also needed to be just right. Paul Davies explains:

> The large-scale structure and motion of the universe is equally remarkable. The accumulated gravity of the universe operates to restrain the expansion, causing it to decelerate with time. In the primeval phase the expansion was much faster than it is today. The universe is thus the product of a competition between the explosive vigor of the big bang, and the force of gravity which tries to pull the pieces back together again. In recent years, astrophysicists have come to realize just how delicately this competition has been balanced. Had the big bang been weaker, the cosmos would have soon fallen back on itself in a big crunch. On the other hand, had it been stronger, the cosmic material would have dispersed so rapidly that galaxies would not have formed. Either way, the observed structure of the universe seems to depend very sensitively on the precise matching of explosive vigor to gravitating power. Just how sensitively is revealed by calculation. At the so-called Planck time (10^{-43} seconds) (which is the earliest moment at which the concept of space and time has meaning) the matching was accurate to a staggering one part in 10^{60}. That is to say, had the explosion differed in strength at the outset by only one part in 10^{60}, the universe we now perceive would not exist. To give some meaning to these numbers, suppose you wanted to fire a bullet at a one-inch target on the other side of the observable universe, twenty billion years away. Your aim would have to be accurate to that same part in 10^{60}.[7]

It does look fixed. It looks intended. It looks as if there was a decision made that it was important to have life in this universe. And there are so many factors that need to be managed: the order of the universe needed vast quantities of negative entropy; the lack of black holes, which one would expect to dominate a chaotic universe; the uniform structure and behavior of the universe beyond the light horizon; and the fundamental constraints of nature (i.e., those basic entities that have the same numerical value throughout the universe and across all time). As Paul Davies sums up: "There seems to be no obvious reason why the universe did not go berserk, expanding in a chaotic and uncoordinated way, producing enormous black holes. Channeling the explosive violence into such a regular and organized pattern of motion seems like a miracle."[8]

The term "Anthropic Principle" has been created to partly explain this exceptional order that makes life possible. Coined originally by the astrophysicist Brandon Carter in 1973, the Principle suggests that all the remarkable variables in the universe have precisely the right values for life to appear. The Anthropic Principle suggests strongly that we were always intended: it looks like we were expected. Since Brandon Carter, an impressive literature has been generated. It was John Barrow and Frank Tipler who wrote the classic *The Anthropic Cosmological Principle*.[9] Since then, Paul Davies, Martin Rees,[10] and Stephen Hawkins[11] have made substantial contributions to the debate. Probably the finest analysis of the philosophy of the debate is Rodney D. Holder's *God, the Multiverse, and Everything*.[12]

It is worth stressing that none of this data has anything to do with the "intelligent design" hypothesis. Intelligent design is a version of creationism that assumes that there are certain gaps, where a direct divine act is necessary to enable the chain that produced life on Earth possible. The data we are considering here is the mathematics of the universe that is so remarkable that it seems to suggest that an agent was underpinning the chain (although not breaking into the chain). It is data that all physicists (Christian or otherwise) accept.

It is fun looking at how Richard Dawkins handled all this data. He is a good enough scientist to know that it is true. He concedes that this universe does look as if life was intended. Dawkins comments on Martin Rees and the way that the six fundamental constraints for life needed to be exactly right and writes: "The bottom line for each of them is the same. The actual number sits in a Goldilocks band of values outside which life would not have been possible."[13] Now, by "Goldilocks band," Dawkins is referring to the remarkable fortuitous nature of the nature. So how does he make sense of it? He starts by excluding a priori the concept of a God who intended life to emerge. He rejects this for the rather muddled reason that anything as complex as a God would have to be an end result of a physical process (see chapter 1 for why this is muddled). He then moves on to suggest that the term "anthropic principle" should be used to describe the skeptic's alternative to theism. So Dawkins writes:

> We have the theist's answer on the one hand, and the anthropic answer on the other. The theist says that God, when setting up the universe, tuned the fundamental constants of the universe so that each one lay in its Goldilocks zone for the production of life. It is as though God had six knobs that he could twiddle and he carefully tuned each knob to its Goldilocks value. As ever, the theist's answer is deeply unsatisfying, because it leaves the existence of God unexplained.[14]

So, in what sense is the anthropic answer the alternative? Dawkins uses the term to describe the "magic of large numbers."[15] To explain the remarkable achievement of lifeless matter becoming life on Earth, Dawkins reminds us that we live in a vast universe where at least one planet (probably more) will enable the factors to create life to come together. Couple that, he explains, with the distinctive crane of Darwinian evolution and the God hypothesis is not needed.

Let us concede for a moment that the millions of planets in this universe might make the improbable (i.e., the emergence of life from lifeless matter) possible. How does he explain the fact that at the cosmological level – across the entire universe – the constants are precisely what are needed to produce life? Dawkins opts for the multiverse theory. This is the claim that there is a portfolio of universes (all of which exist) and we just happen to be in the one that mathematically enables life to emerge. Naturally, we are not in a position to exist in any of the other universes. Hugh Everett in 1957 postulated the "parallel universe" theory to explain the quantum measurement paradox. This involves the universe splitting as a result of an electron to enable two options to be realized simultaneously. With physicists postulating multiple universes in one domain, it seems attractive to suggest that there are many (perhaps an infinite number) of universes, of which only a small number produce life. So, as Paul Davies puts it, "The multiverse theory seeks to replace the appearance of design by the hand of chance."[16] Paul Davies argues that this is a legitimate scientific theory and evidence to support this hypothesis may come by looking at the precise mathematical rules surrounding the chance.

Paul Davies becomes almost surreal as he discusses the details of the multiverse hypothesis. He suggests that it may extend to "fake universes" (such as the one explored in the movie the *Matrix*). Now, I suspect Dawkins knows that this is difficult ground for him. Unlike the explanation for life on Earth, we do at least know about the millions upon millions of other planets in this universe. We know that these other planets exist. We also know about the remarkable processes underpinning natural selection. But we do not know about any other universes. And Dawkins concedes that the cosmological data is harder for him to explain than the challenge of life on Earth. Dawkins writes:

> We don't yet have an equivalent crane for physics. Some kind of multiverse theory could in principle do for physics the same explanatory work as Darwinism does for biology. This kind of explanation is superficially less satisfying than the biological version of Darwinism, because it makes heavier demands on luck.[17]

Even for Dawkins, physicists are far removed from the brazen conceit of Laplace. The two serious contenders to explain the exceptional math of the universe are: either an agency that intended life to emerge (the God hypothesis); or millions upon millions of other universes, most of which don't generate life. It is worth pausing and thinking about how extraordinary the multiverse hypothesis is. On this view, this vast universe is not the only one there is. The skeptic now has a view of the world that makes the Christian picture of heaven (the other major universe that Christians postulate) seem rather unimaginative. For the skeptic to evade this remarkable math, he or she needs to postulate millions of other universes (none of which are linked to our space and time); and, in almost all of these universes, life did not emerge because of a variable, which was insufficiently precise. So some have planets but most do not. Most presumably are vast swirling masses of energy. All are vast. And there are millions of these universes. To provide the "magic of large numbers" there needs to be an infinity of such universes. As Rodney Holder observes:

> It is worth contemplating for a moment what we are being asked to swallow if we are to believe in a multiverse. Let us ignore for a moment the measure zero problem and assume that a positive fraction of universes is life-baring. Of the minute proportion bearing any resemblance to ours, there will be some in which an "I", vitually identical with me up to now, fell under a bus completing this chapter; some where there is even more unimaginable evil and suffering than in this one; some where conditions are benign and Eden-like; some in which gorgons or unicorns or wyverns actually exist; and so on, and so on. Just trying to contemplate the infinitely many universes makes us realize how bizarre the hypothesis is.[18]

Now, on what basis can I argue that theism is a better explanation than the multiverse hypothesis? One important philosophical principle is "prior probability." Some years ago, I was standing in the kitchen and noticed some cookie crumbs on the floor. When I confronted my ten-year-old son with the evidence and implied that he was surreptitiously taking a cookie, he offered the alternative explanation of an "alien." Now this explanation is possible, but not probable. As Dawkins would concede, it is possible that aliens exist and perhaps these aliens are interested in cookies. However, the more likely explanation was the appetite of a ten-year-old boy. Unlike aliens, I was sure that the boy exists. I was disinclined to multiply entities to explain the cookie evidence. So by analogy, we do know about the remarkable math of this universe that intended life. When we encounter "intention" in the universe, we normally explain it in terms of agency. We do not postulate unknown and inaccessible universes to provide an explanation for this exceptional math. The principle of Ockham's razor (always opt for the hypothesis which is the simplest explanation for the data) would challenge the multiverse theory.

It is odd that Dawkins is so enthusiastic about the multiverse theory. It does not look like a scientific explanation. Indeed, it has a certain similarity to forms of creationism that Dawkins abhors so much. Holden writes:

> Because of its lack of observable consequences, the appeal to a multiverse provides a metaphysical explanation for life rather than a scientific one. But the theory is also unscientific in another sense. This is because it provides a "catch-all" kind of explanation.
>
> Multiverse theories remind me of the argument put forward by Christian fundamentalist Philip Henry Gosse in the nineteenth century to reconcile a literal reading of Genesis with geology. Nature is really cyclical and God created it instantaneously in mid-cycle – Adam with a naval, trees in Eden appearing to be 50 years old, fossil birds with half-digested food in their stomachs! Anything can be explained on this basis and no observation can possibly contradict the theory. Multiverse theories are equally sterile. Yes, they explain everything, by the simple formula, "If it can happen, it will happen somewhere sometime, so don't be surprised!". But they cannot be falsified: they are completely insensitive to the empirical facts. This is a far cry from the normal kind of explanation sought in science.[19]

The multiverse theory is deeply unsatisfying. It is implausible that there are so many universes; it is unscientific; and it lacks the simplicity of agency and intention.

The climate in physics is now changing the climate in philosophy. Since Bertrand Russell (the philosophical equivalent of Dawkins) the world has changed considerably. Russell's philosophical successor as atheist was Anthony Flew, who has recently announced that he now believes in God. And one of the reasons for this decision is the remarkable evidence around the anthropic principle.

Anthony Flew

It is worth looking at Anthony Flew in more detail. Anthony Flew was the philosopher at the heart of the debates on religious language. He was the person who posed the problem of evil with precision and compelling clarity. His *Presumption of Atheism* was highly acclaimed. He was involved as the atheist representative in the debate with William Lane Craig in 1988. This debate was promoted as the re-run of the debate between Bertrand Russell and Frederic Copleston, which was held in 1948.

It is interesting to compare these two debates. For Russell and Copleston, science is much more of a problem for faith. For Craig and Flew, science is more of a problem for atheism. As Paul Badham notes in his discussion of the two debates:

> The essential difference between the Russell–Copleston debate and the Craig–Flew debate is the shift in scientific opinion about the nature of the Universe which has occurred in the intervening years. Bertrand Russell lived at a time when scientists assumed that the universe was eternal and hence uncaused. Consequently, when Copleston tried to argue for the universe being created, Russell could just sit back, fold his arms and declare, "the Universe is just there, and that's all". . . . Now however the situation is totally different because the consensus of contemporary science is that the Universe has not always existed. It came into being from nothing between twelve and fifteen billion years ago. Moreover scientists also believe that the initial condition of the Universe immediately after the "Big Bang" appears to be "finely tuned" for the emergence of life and mind. This looks like design.[20]

Flew finds it difficult to respond to the science in Craig's arguments. He opts for agnosticism and reiterates David Hume's principle that metaphysics is just inaccessible. Flew in this debate felt that any attempt to "know" what caused the universe is "too bold."[21] (Knowledge and boldness are subjects we will return to in the last chapter.) And he spends much of his time taking issue with other aspects of Craig's theology. So Flew complains:

> He [i.e., Craig] goes on to indicate that "No orthodox Christian *likes* the doctrine of hell or delights in anyone's condemnation. I truly wish that universalism were true, but it is not." Well, I regard that as a sign of grace, that he says that, but I still have to say that these two things are simply incompatible – it's a nightmare.[22]

These two responses to Craig's arguments left Flew vulnerable. First, it is not true that humans cannot explore the origins of the universe – physicists are doing an excellent job. And the data that physicists are discovering does require an explanation – hence the two primary options of theism or a multiverse. And, second, Craig's enthusiasm for hell is not an argument against the existence of God. Additionally, there are plenty of Christians who would want to discuss, and take issue with, the nature of God's judgment with Craig.

Perhaps this debate was a factor in Flew's change of mind. However, Flew's shift supports Badham's observation that science is less a problem for religious faith now and more of a problem for atheism. In fact, the primary reason for Flew's move to "deism" was the data emerging from cosmologists. And the heart of Flew's argument is that the scientific picture of the world is so different. He writes:

> Imagine entering a hotel room on your next vacation. The CD player on the bedside table is softly playing a track from your favorite recording. The framed print over the bed is identical to the image that hangs over the fireplace at home. The room is scented with your favorite fragrance. You shake your head in amazement and drop your bags on the floor.
>
> You're suddenly very alert. You step over to the minibar, open the door, and stare at wonder at the contents. Your favorite beverages. Your favorite cookies and candy. Even the brand of bottled water you prefer.
>
> You turn from the minibar, then, and gaze around the room. You notice the book on the desk: it's the latest volume by your favorite author. You glance into the bathroom, where personal care

and grooming products are lined up on the counter, each one as if it was chosen specifically for you. You switch on the television; it is tuned to your favorite channel.

Chances are, with each new discovery about your hospitable new environment, you would be less inclined to think it were all a mere coincidence, right? You might wonder how the hotel managers acquired such detailed information about you. You might marvel at their meticulous preparation. You might even double-check what all this is going to cost you. But you would certainly be inclined to believe that someone knew you were coming.[23]

Although Flew describes this as a "clumsy" parallel to the argument emerging from modern science, it captures the central issue very well. The coincidences are so remarkable that even the skeptics feel that some explanation is needed. So, instead of postulating a hotel manager who organized the room knowing that you would be in that room, they are postulating a vast hotel with millions upon millions of rooms – one of which is, rather fortuitously, perfect for the guest.

The multiverse hypothesis has already been examined and found wanting for a variety of good reasons. However, Flew observes that even if the multiverse hypothesis was right, then there is still a question that requires explanation. He writes:

What is especially important here is the fact that the existence of a multiverse does not explain the origin of the laws of nature . . . So multiverse or not, we still have to come to terms with the origins of the laws of nature. And the only viable explanation here is the divine Mind.[24]

In one sense, at this point Flew is simply revisiting the cosmological arguments of Aquinas. Dawkins is fixated on the question: who made God? In so doing, he often does not really understand the arguments that he is describing and examining. And the cosmological argument is a good example.

The cosmological argument has a long and complex history. We find it embedded in the writings of Aristotle (384 BCE– 322 BCE) and made famous by Aristotle's thirteenth-century admirer, Aquinas (1225–74). The key question underpinning the cosmological argument (especially the third of Aquinas's five ways) is: why does anything exist?

A scientist is a person who seeks explanations. It is a basic principle of science that the world is intelligible (even the very paradoxical world of sub-atomic particles can be mapped with math). When something is, the scientist asks the question "why"? This incredible universe and for now let us imagine it includes billions of multiverses are all subject to certain basic laws of nature. So why is this? What is the explanation for these basic laws?

If this universe is ultimately intelligible, then an explanation is needed. And the whole point of the cosmological argument is that the explanation must be something other than the universe. Or, to use Aquinas's language, a universe is not intelligible if it is simply a collection of contingent explanations (and by contingent, I mean an explanation that could be otherwise). Take any event (say, a tree falling over and blocking a road), as we seek to understand the why (a gale, which in turn was called by the hurricane arising off the coast, which in turn is caused by the weather system of the Earth), slowly we will find ourselves pushed back to the fundamental laws of nature embedded in the universe. If our instincts are that the universe is intelligible, then any explanation for these fundamental laws must be "necessary" (the opposite of contingent, i.e., the explanation must contain within itself the reason for its own existence – it must be self-explanatory). The concept of God as developed in the monotheist traditions is one that is necessary (a being that is ultimately self-explanatory). It is of a different character to the physical explanations within the universe. And the creator of the universe is the explanation for the fundamental laws of nature that (perhaps) underpinning every universe that is.

Now Dawkins et al. can retort that they don't believe the universe is ultimately intelligible. But they must be careful. This is the route that Nietzsche took. They could argue that perhaps the universe is only intelligible in a small local way or that the intelligibility consists of mental construct imposed on chaotic sense data. However, science as a discipline would not want to take either route. And, given the remarkable explanatory power of science, the intelligibility of the universe does not seem to be either local or simply a mental construct imposed on experience. The very assumption of science seems to vindicate the instinct of theism. As events within the universe are explained and understood, so the universe (or universes) as a whole can be explained and understood. It is the result of the act of creation by a God who is a necessary being.

To Sum Up

In the last two chapters we have seen how the gift of faith is analogous to the gift of sight. It is the capacity to see the transcendent in the immanent (in the same way one picture can be both an old woman and a young woman). It is the capacity to see the divine in one's experience of the world. In the same way as sight or smell or the learning of a language needs to be cultivated (it takes time to appreciate great art or discern the smell of grass in a full New Zealand Sauvignon Blanc wine), so the capacity to see God needs to be nurtured.

Although the heart of faith is grounded in this direct experience of the world, the vision of a world intended by an act of love is justified by a variety of arguments. In this chapter, we have seen how physics has "matured" from the conceit of Laplace into the complexity of a discourse that takes the possibility of God seriously. The speculation of parallel universes (many millions of them occupying vast quantities of space) makes Christian musings of a "heaven" seem positively parochial. And, as we will see in chapter 8, the discourse of deep connectivity across the universe at the sub-atomic level makes Christian accounts of prayer possible. Modern physics is definitely faith-friendly. Biology is not yet in this place. And Richard Dawkins is behaving just like Laplace. He is understandably proud of the impressive strides that his discipline is making. For this reason, it is going through its teenage phase as a discipline.

As we have seen, the discussion of physics in the *God Delusion* illustrates this tension between physics and biology. Dawkins is frustrated that there is not a similar "crane" to Darwinian natural selection in physics. Dawkins admits the remarkable data emerging from astrophysicists about the mathematics of the universe. The "fine-tuning" argument is a good argument for faith: the simplest explanation for the ways in which this universe clearly intended life to emerge is to recognize there is an agent capable of agency. This is the natural explanation for agency.

And, finally, it was Anthony Flew who took us back to the cosmological argument. Even if there are billions of universes (and we just happen to be in the only life-friendly one), we still need to determine whether the basic scientific intuition is justified. Is the universe ultimately intelligible? If the answer is yes, then the ultimate explanation for the universe must be something other than the physical and must contain within itself the reason for its own existence (a central characteristic of the concept of a creator). If the answer is no, then the very intuition of science is undermined.

Cultivating the religious sense should be seen as not simply compatible with science, but as arising out of science. God can be found both at the level of the discoveries in physics and in the very intuitions underpinning science.

However, we now need to learn what this God is like. For this, we now turn to that much maligned book, the Bible, and the hard work of theology.

5

A Revealing God

Dawkins and Hitchens (Harris less so) tend to see the world going from primitive and stupid to enlightened and scientific. No effort is made to read the Bible or the Qur'an within its context or to recognize the singular achievement of the text given its time. Instead, from the vantage point of privilege (for Dawkins as he sits inside the Senior Common Room in Oxford University), the text is judged as if it is a paper written by an Oxford undergraduate and is failed outright.

Religious people are not stupid. And there are countless thoughtful strategies that engage with these texts in all their complexities. We do not need Hitchens, Harris, and Dawkins to describe the text to us: we know that Abraham – a father – almost kills his son Isaac; we know there are passages where God seems to command the genocide of an entire nation or people; and we are deeply aware that there are passages that have been used to justify intolerance and injustice. Indeed, there have been countless engagements with these difficult passages – all of which our three atheists were too lazy to discover.

So, in this chapter, we are going to explore the claims that a person of faith wants to make for Scripture. As with the entire book, it will be written from a Christian perspective, but one that takes seriously the reality of religious pluralism.

Working within Certain Limitations

One reason why atheists find religion puzzling is that they disregard certain limitations that are built into the knowing process. As we see at the start of chapter 3, knowing is necessarily local. And this is an important theme of this book, so let us revisit that theme here. We learn a language within a family; we are introduced to a certain way of looking at the world; we inherit certain customs and practices; and we learn through the texts, ideas, and people we meet. No one has instant access to all knowledge that has emerged in every culture. Even in an Internet age, this is still impossible. It is impossible because a great deal of knowledge depends on being formed within a culture; Chinese atonal music, for example, requires the living within that culture for appreciation to be possible. Even "propositional knowledge," concerning facts about the world, depends on learning languages and seeing how systems link together. It all takes considerable time.

We learn from the reality of this universe that God takes the long view. Although God could have created the entire universe in seven days, we know that God did not choose this option. Contrary to our culture of impatience and instant satisfaction, God wanted a process in which planets formed and stars died. As human evolved, God was willing to work within the limitations placed on human communities. Human ingenuity would make discoveries over time. And a discovery (for example, the wheel) would slowly spread to other cultures. Although we could imagine a different universe where knowledge would spread more rapidly, this is a universe where family and community are central. Growing up with parents and siblings and knowing them well is a very effective way of introducing the primary discovery that God wants us to learn – the discovery of giving and receiving love. Of course, this means that countless generations have not enjoyed antibiotics (and suffered as a result), but again from the divine perspective, the canvas is much larger. This life is located in the context of eternity; this life is never intended to be everything.

So God determined certain constraints for knowing that made it inevitable that even knowledge of God would be subject to the same constraint. Martyn Percy is right, "The Bible is not a fax sent down by God."[1] And, of course, a fax would be impossible to send: the technology didn't exist until the twentieth century and required the formation of a community that would understand such a disclosure from God and be able to spread the discoveries around the world.

So, once this is recognized, then the following picture starts to emerge. It is not a picture of moving from primitive (and more misguided) to advanced (and therefore more enlightened). Indeed, one could argue that the indigenous religious traditions of the world have more insight than the sophisticated scientific worldview of the West. Without over-sentimentalizing these sophisticated traditions, there are remarkable insights that seem to be shared across vast geographical distances. There is a shared reverence for the world. There is a heightened "religious sense" radiating through these traditions. As John Mbiti puts it, "For African peoples, this is a religious universe. Nature in the broadest sense of the word is not an empty impersonal object or phenomenon: it is filled with religious significance."[2] This worldview is shared with Native Americans. And, in both traditions, there are certain implications that are worthy of careful study by the modern West. For example, we could learn from their emphasis on the "respect" for, and the interconnectedness of, everything. In this area, these indigenous traditions are perhaps ahead of the modern West.

Each culture formed a different description of the "spirit" world and the way in which it intersected with the physical world. However, even in this realm, we discover certain themes that proved very important for the development of religion. There is a monotheism in almost all these traditions. Although there are often many deities, there is normally one that transcends the others. And these traditions are very careful to distinguish "God" from the creation. So John Mbiti writes, "African peoples acknowledge the omnipresence of God. He may be in the thunder, but he is not thunder; he may shoot forth like a waterfall, but he is not the waterfall; he may be associated with the sky, but he is not identical with it."[3]

It is important to appreciate the centrality of ritual in these indigenous traditions. Religions do not consist of just beliefs, but of a whole complex set of practices, which are expressed in elaborate rituals. We learn through doing. From the outside, some of these practices can seem bizarre. And of course this is universally true: some of the practices in Oxford colleges will appear bizarre from the outside. One Native American practice that looks odd from the outside is the sun dance. The Oglala Lakota, for example, have a sun dance, which can involve over four days of dancing with very little food or water. However, from the inside the practice is deeply profound. And, of course, the "sun dance" recognizes an important "scientific truth", namely, the importance of the sun for human survival.

From the vantage point of anthropology or sociology, one might just see these beliefs as an example of the human capacity to interpret the world in a certain way, and the practices as rites that bind a community together. And, on a certain level, these accounts are true. From the vantage point of faith, however, these beliefs and practices are the result of God putting pressure on the human consciousness to cultivate a religious sensitivity and to start the process of discerning how best to interpret that realm.

Now these indigenous traditions are almost all "oral" cultures. It was through the telling of stories that the insights were disseminated from generation to generation. For God to provide a fuller disclosure, God would need humanity to master the art of writing. And this occurred in several traditions. However, for our purposes, we shall concentrate on the discoveries within Judaism, which then birthed Christianity and Islam.

The Emergence of the Hebrew Scriptures

The world owes a massive debt to Judaism. This small tradition has had a remarkable impact on the history of ideas. Much like the indigenous traditions, the Jewish traditions start as stories, which are passed from generation to generation. But a key theme of the tradition is the oneness and unity of God.

This is the realm of pre-history. However, according to Jewish tradition, a key person is Abraham. And, insofar as we can date Abraham, it is approximately 1800 BCE, when Abraham responds to the call and creates a people who recognize that the source of everything is Yahweh. The stories of Abraham would start to be written down about 800 years later, during the period of the monarchy. And the text that emerged from these stories makes up the Hebrew Bible, which is, for Christians, the Old Testament.

With any ancient text, one cannot treat it in the same way as a book written by a colleague at Oxford University. One wants to treat the texts in the past as one hopes that the future will treat texts of today. So, for example, from afar the creation story can look rather odd: here are two people – Adam and Eve – persuaded by a serpent to eat an apple in a garden, which makes God very upset. However, when one is closer to the text, one cannot help but marvel at the sophistication of the narrative.

It all starts with that powerful declaration that "in the beginning, God created the heavens and the earth." The primary vehicle of God's creation is the spoken word. "Then God said, 'Let there be light'" (Genesis 1: 3). One is misunderstanding the text if one imagines a big mouth issuing an edict for light to be. Instead, the idea here is that in the same way as words are an expression of thoughts, so the creation is an expression of the thought of God. It is a poetic expression of the truth that everything emerges as a result of divine agency and decision.

As a narrative, it breaks through and deconstructs many features of creation stories that were dominant in other cultures. So, in Genesis, we do not find the battle with a cosmic opponent or the struggle with recalcitrant matter. Here the serpent in Genesis 2 and 3 is not standing alongside God, but under the control of God. It does not advocate a cosmic dualism (two equal and opposite forces battling it out in creation). God creates *ex nihilo* (out of nothing); it is a God which is sovereign and in control. There is nothing primitive about Genesis: it can speak "truth" to our age as it has always done.

Naturally, the text works with the scientific model that was prevalent in the author's day. The theological truth is captured in a narrative with a particular scientific model operating. So it seems that there is a dome across the sky, which separates the waters in the skies from the waters on the Earth. Given light is created on the first day and the sun created on the fourth day, the sun is not understood to be the source of the light. Instead, it is seen as a lamp hanging inside the dome to provide light for Earth during the day. So the text is assuming a pre-modern cosmology. At this point, Dawkins and Hitchens might want to make an issue of this fact. However, it could not be otherwise. It could not be otherwise because the text would be unintelligible to the people who created the text unless it worked with their scientific worldview. But it also could not be otherwise because when it comes to the universe we are always working with models. We are very conscious of how, over the last hundred years, the Newtonian model of the universe has been modified by the work of Albert Einstein. God, who does know the truth about the science of the universe, could not impart that truth to us because we would not have understood it.

But the point of the narrative is not the pre-modern cosmology about domes and firmament. The point of the narrative is that God is the source of everything that is and sustains everything that is. The image of the Word being the vehicle of creation invites us to see the creation as a revelation of the nature of God. So, for example, as we look at the power within creation, we recognize that this reflects, in a limited way, the power of the Creator. As a Christian, I affirm unequivocally the truth of the Genesis narrative. I affirm the theological truths capture in the narrative.

So I am absolutely clear, the truth of Genesis is completely compatible with the narrative emerging from modern science. All truth is part of God's truth. The basic shape of Darwin's hypothesis has survived critical scrutiny. There is no scientist of repute working in a British or major American university who would quarrel with the main outline. The main difference is that we are now clearer as to the mechanism: we have discovered that the main player in the development of life is DNA mutation. Arthur Peacocke sums up neo-Darwinian evolution in two ideas: "all organisms past, present and future, descend from earlier living systems, the first of which arose spontaneously; and species are derived from one another by natural selection of the best procreators."[4] In other words, life on Planet Earth is linked together; subsequent species emerged from earlier ones, and in particular humanity is related to apes. As a scientific hypothesis, this has been established beyond all reasonable doubt.

Notice how two factors come together. The first is that the achievement of the text should be recognized. Although it was written working with a particular pre-modern cosmology, one can easily recognize as true the poetic truth beyond the cosmology. The truth of the narrative is less a description of the past and more a claim about the presence – the sense that the claim that God has enabled everything to be, and sustains everything, is as true now as it was at the origins of everything. The second factor is that we need to recognize and accommodate the discoveries that modern science is making. Although there are important questions posed to faith by neo-Darwinian evolution, I cannot evade those questions by denial of the scientific consensus.

A similar approach should be taken to chapters 2 and 3 of Genesis – the story of Adam and Eve. A close reading of the text reveals a different tradition, which is probably older than the tradition in Genesis 1, underpinning this narrative. It seems to retell the story of creation, but this time, unlike chapter 1, starting with the creation of humanity. Once again, it is easy for our atheist readers of the text to overlook the many layers. And this text needs to be read with care.

Traditionally, Christians have seen this as a straightforward "Fall." Adam and Eve in an act of disobedience reject the idyllic environment that God had provided them. Augustine of Hippo, for example, for the brilliant Bishop of Hippo, seeks to distinguish very firmly between the perfect creation that a good God made and the exercise of angelic (in the form of a fallen angel, the serpent) and human freewill. For Augustine, God made this perfect world, which humans then spoiled by the exercise of human freedom in a sinful way.

In the same way as science is not a static narrative – otherwise our biology would have stopped with Aristotle's classifications of nature – neither is theology. For a contrasting reading of the text, Anne Primavesi – the feminist theologian – sees the narrative as a "growing up" rather than a "Fall."

In Genesis 2 and 3, Primavesi argues, God is more like a potter engaged in the process of creation. The creation of the male is firmly linked to the world; there is a deliberate Hebrew word-play – God creates an "earthling (or human) of clods from the Earth (or humus)." There is no hierarchical male lording it over woman and the rest of creation. Instead, the male shares with the rest of the created order the same substance and spirit. The image of God in the text is odd. God permits Adam and Eve to enjoy the garden save for the tree of the knowledge of good and evil. The text seems to suggest that God wants Adam and Eve to live in perpetual immaturity – like children who never grow up. In fact, suggests Primavesi, God comes out of the text rather badly. She writes:

> God appears as a rather benevolent, albeit tyrannical male parent, kind enough to give his children life, a cosy existence and suitable playmates. In return he demands total obedience from them, under constant supervision. They are denied basic human liberties: the knowledge of good and evil and freedom of choice. God secures their obedience by threats.[5]

For Primavesi, it is clear that in the disagreement between the serpent and God, God does not tell the truth. Both the serpent and God describe the consequences of eating the fruit from the tree of knowledge of good and evil. (She notes in passing that elsewhere in the Hebrew Bible knowledge of good and evil is a virtue; God, for example, praises Solomon who asks that he may "discern between good and evil", 1 Kings 3: 9.) So "the Lord God commanded the man, 'You may freely eat of every tree of the garden; but of the tree of the knowledge of good and evil you shall not eat, for in the day that you eat of it you shall die'" (Genesis 2: 16–17). So the punishment is "death" on the day the fruit is eaten. Now the serpent disagrees. The text reads: "But the serpent said to the woman, 'You will not die; for God knows that when you eat of it your eyes will be opened, and you will be like God, knowing good and evil'" (Genesis 3: 4–5). And, at the end of chapter 3, God says: "See, the man has become like one of us, knowing good and evil; and now, he might reach out his hand and take also from the tree of life, and eat, and live for ever" (Genesis 3: 22). To Primavesi, it is clear. God is insisting on moral immaturity and makes a threat to keep humanity in that place. The serpent explains to Eve that humanity will not die, but instead have a moral awareness like God. And at the end of the chapter, God seems to concede that humanity has a moral awareness.

At this point, note how we are really struggling with the text. And the Christian tradition at its best does this: this is how a person of faith, following in the footsteps of Augustine of Hippo and Thomas Aquinas, operates. It might be easier for Hitchens and Dawkins to spend their time with the "young earth Creationists," but if they really are going to undermine Christianity, they need to work with the finest theological reflection and not the worst. Primavesi suggests that instead of a "Fall" we have a "growing up." In my judgment, Paul Tillich offers an account of this narrative that is both faithful to the complexity of the text and theologically sensitive. And one aspect of the text that Primavesi does not take sufficiently seriously is the context: Genesis 1–3 is immediately followed by a tragic descent into murder, mayhem (culminating in the Flood), and evil. So there is clearly a "Fall" intended in the narrative, which results in "sin" in all its complexity and wickedness.

So Tillich starts by stressing the point made earlier that Genesis 1–3 is less a text about the past and more a text about the present. So, from Genesis 1, we learn that God is the enabler and sustainer of the creation. From Genesis 2 and 3, we learn that we are in constant tension with the Creator. He would concur with Primavesi that there is inevitability in this struggle – or, to use his language, "sin is made ontologically necessary."[6] In other words, the text is inviting us to recognize that some sort of human autonomy is essential as we strive for moral awareness. It remains an act of disobedience, but it is an inevitable and necessary act of disobedience. In the same way as teenagers necessarily and inevitably push back on their parents, so all of humanity forms our identity by pushing back on God. However, this pushing back carries significant risk and dangers: it can lead to hubris, where we start denying any need for a creator, and to an unregulated sense of desire. It can lead to murder, mayhem, and wickedness.

The power of Genesis 1–3 is that it captures the human reality perfectly. We are made and enabled by God to be. We are also able to exercise our human freedom and, as we started to define ourselves, that freedom was exercised. However, we are constantly in danger of exercising that freedom in deeply destructive ways – ways that can destroy self, those around us, and the environment that we live in.

Judaism gave to the world this remarkable text. We have seen how the text speaks deeply and powerfully to the human condition. We have also seen how important it is to read the text closely and in conversation with a tradition of inquiry. Augustine of Hippo, a Church Father, has been placed in conversation with a contemporary feminist theologian. The result is a reading that is faithful to the text and "theologically" sensitive.

Now, at this point, Dawkins objects thus: "The ethnic cleansing begun in the time of Moses is brought to bloody fruition in the book of Joshua, a text remarkable for the bloodthirsty massacres it records and the xenophobic relish with which it does so."[7] And it is appropriate for Dawkins to draw our attention to the problem passages that are morally obscene. What about the passages where the Lord God commands a complete destruction of a people? This is a good question. And so we turn to the book of Deuteronomy. It reads:

> When the LORD your God brings you into the land that you are about to enter and occupy, and he clears away many nations before you – the Hittites, the Girgashites, the Amorites, the Canaanites, the Perizzites, the Hivites, and the Jebusites, seven nations mightier and more numerous than you – and when the LORD your God gives them over to you and you defeat them, then you must utterly destroy them. Make no covenant with them and show them no mercy. Do not intermarry with them, giving your daughters to

their sons or taking their daughters for your sons, for that would turn away your children from following me, to serve other gods. Then the anger of the LORD would be kindled against you, and he would destroy you quickly. But this is how you must deal with them: break down their altars, smash their pillars, hew down their sacred poles, and burn their idols with fire. For you are a people holy to the LORD your God; the LORD your God has chosen you out of all the peoples on Earth to be his people, his treasured possession. (Deuteronomy 7: 1–7)

It is so important to read a text closely and on a number of different levels. There is a level of complex history. Probably the settlement of Palestine was a slow and gradual process, which occurred in 1300 BCE. Although the data around the Exodus out of Egypt is difficult to confirm, the centrality of the story makes it highly likely that we have a people fleeing oppression and suffering. Here we have a homeless people searching for a home. Here we have a people trusting that the God who liberated them from Egypt will enable them to find that home. On another level, we have a whole set of traditions that seek to justify this command by God. So, for example, much is made of the pre-Israelite practice of child sacrifice that did occur in this part of the world before the Israelites arrived. It is argued in the text that these practices provoked this commandment by God.

However, it is interesting to look at the text more closely. The distinguished scholar of the Old Testament, Walter Moberly, has noted how the injunction "to destroy them and show them no mercy" is immediately followed by a commandment not to marry any of them. What we have here is the self-correcting nature of the Hebrew Bible. The sense that God ordered the genocide of a people is modified to stress the importance of holiness (being separate and being faithful to the God of Israel). The injunction not to intermarry means that God's commandment to destroy all the people has not been carried out. Instead, the tradition has corrected itself: the real point here is not the genocide of an entire people, but the importance of faithfulness. For the ancient mind, it is not necessary to repeal explicitly the first commandment; they sit together in deliberate shocking paradox.

Now the obvious question is: did God command the genocide of a people or not? It is a point that Dawkins enjoys making. Dawkins writes:

> Yet again, theologians will protest, it didn't happen. . . . The point is that, whether true or not, the Bible is held up to us as the source of our morality. And the Bible story of Joshua's destruction of Jericho, and the invasion of the Promised Land in general, is morally indistinguishable from Hitler's invasion of Poland, or Saddam Hussein's massacres of the Kurds and the Marsh Arabs. The Bible may be an arresting and poetic work of fiction, but it is not the sort of book you should give your children to form their morals.[8]

Leaving to one side the fact that Dawkins is being lazy – so he ignores the "child-sacrifice issue" and draws a comparison between an ancient practice and a twentieth-century one, involving Hitler and Saddam Hussein (where the culprits were both secularist, that is, non-practicing religious people) – the question remains. Did God order a genocide (even if it didn't occur)?

And the answer is that God did not, for reasons that are constantly affirmed throughout the Hebrew Bible. Elsewhere in the Hebrew Bible, it is God who calls Israel's neighbors to discover better ways of organizing themselves (see, for example, the opening chapter of Amos). In the book of Ruth, we see how the faith of the outsider is constantly affirmed (Ruth is from Moab). The overall witness of the Hebrew Bible is that God cares for all people. And the very fact that the narrative here in Deuteronomy corrects itself is clear evidence that the tradition is aware of the incompatibility arising from the command to commit genocide.

The revelation of the nature of God is not found in one particular verse or text. It is found pulsating through the text in its entirety. Scripture contains the word of God, but there are sentences within the text that are misinterpretations of the will of God. The literal injunction to commit genocide is an example of a misinterpretation of the will of God.

The insights that Judaism provided for the world formed the basis for the emergence of two other major faith traditions – Christianity and Islam. In the next chapter, we shall examine Christianity and in chapter 7 Islam.

6

Christianity

For Christopher Hitchens, the work of Bart Ehrman has helpfully explained the extraordinary worldview of Jesus, which makes the claims of Christianity very implausible. Hitchens contrasts Ehrman with C. S. Lewis and commends Ehrman on his careful study of the New Testament. "Fluent in Greek and Hebrew," Hitchens writes, "he [i.e., Ehrman] eventually could not reconcile his faith with his scholarship."[1] So let us start this exploration of Christianity by looking more closely at the position and arguments of Bart Ehrman.[2]

Bart Ehrman summarizes the worldview of Jesus thus: "Jesus thought that the history of the world would come to a screeching halt, that God would intervene in the affairs of this planet, overthrow the forces of evil in a cosmic act of judgment, and establish his utopian Kingdom here on earth. And this was to happen within Jesus' own generation."[3] Ehrman sets out the evidence for this account of Jesus with some care. First, within first-century Judaism, apocalypticism is widespread. The apocalyptic worldview flourishes in a climate where people are suffering: and the Jewish people who had been forced to cope with endless occupations knew what suffering involved. Provoked by the Romans, in 66 CE there was a revolt that resulted in thousands of Jews in Jerusalem being slaughtered. Given this context, it is not surprising that some Jews "publicly proclaimed the imminent end of their suffering through the supernatural intervention of God."[4] A major group, the Essenes, who were a community seeking to live an appropriately rigorous observant life in the desert (about whom we know a great deal through the Dead Sea Scrolls), believed in the imminent end of the world. So apocalypticism is an important part of the context of Jesus's ministry.

Second, certain passages from Mark's Gospel make perfect sense in this context. Mark's Gospel is important because it is the earliest source for the historical Jesus. So, for example, in Mark's Gospel we find Jesus saying the following:

> "Those who are ashamed of me and of my words in this adulterous and sinful generation, of them the Son of Man will also be ashamed when he comes in the glory of his Father with the holy angels." And he said to them, "Truly I tell you, there are some standing here who will not taste death until they see that the kingdom of God has come with power." (Mark 8: 38–9: 1)

or:

> But in those days, after that suffering, the sun will be darkened, and the moon will not give its light, and the stars will be falling from heaven, and the powers in the heavens will be shaken. Then they will see "the Son of Man coming in clouds" with great power and glory. Then he will send out the angels, and gather his elect from the four winds, from the ends of the earth to the ends of heaven. "From the fig tree learn its lesson: as soon as its branch becomes tender and puts forth its leaves, you know that summer is near. So also, when you see these things taking place, you know that he is near, at the very gates. Truly I tell you, this generation will not pass away until all these things have taken place." (Mark 13: 24–30)

Ehrman is right to argue that there is a consistent apocalyptic worldview that can be assembled from these texts that most likely go back to the historical Jesus. We have a vision of what the rules for the coming reign of God will look like: a "reversal of fortunes"[5] – the values and priorities of the current evil age will be reversed; and "salvation for sinners,"[6] the lost and needy. In addition, Jesus believes in a judgment that is both universal and

imminent.[7] As Ehrman admits, much of this message is in con-
tinuity with the prophetic tradition of the Hebrew Bible, but it
is also different – the Kingdom will be established by a dramatic
act of God. Ehrman summarizes thus:

> [T]his message was like that proclaimed throughout the writings
> of the prophets in the Hebrew Bible. Judgment was coming,
> people needed to repent in preparation or they would be con-
> demned. Those who turned to God, though, would be saved. At
> the same time, Jesus' message was different, for his was framed
> within an apocalyptic context. As a first-century Jew, Jesus lived
> when many Jews expected God to intervene once and for all for
> his people, to overthrow the forces of evil that had gained ascend-
> ancy in the world and to bring in his good Kingdom on earth.
> There would be then be no more war, poverty, disease, calamity,
> sin, hatred, or death. The kingdom would arrive in power, and
> all that was opposed to it would be destroyed and removed.[8]

It is clear then that the message of Jesus was about the reign
of God which will be ushered in through a decisive divine
action. It is also clear that Jesus believed he was the agent of
God that makes it possible for the kingdom to arrive. As Erhman
puts it: "Jesus maintained that people who heard his message
and followed it would enter into the future Kingdom of God. Thus
Jesus portrayed himself as the herald of this Kingdom, who knew
when it was coming and how it would arrive. More than that,
he evidently saw himself as having a special standing before
God. After all, whoever accepted his message would enter God's
Kingdom."[9]

Now, for Bart Ehrman and Christopher Hitchens, the conversation can stop right here. For Ehrman and Hitchens, Jesus is
simply another wacky person who believed the world was going
to end soon and he had an important part to play in that world.
However, I want to suggest that this picture of the apocalyptic
Jesus can be both affirmed and transformed.

The picture can be affirmed in this way. Human society is
constantly on the edge of the apocalypse. It is amazing how we
can let our social lives become so disorderly and damaging. The
claim of the New Testament is that Jesus is the agent of God who

can bring about a transformation that will start now and culmin- ate at the end of the age. Mark's Gospel, for example, is clear: the reign of God has already started and we are all invited to recognize God's rule (see Mark 1: 15). We recognize the author- ity of God when we live a life of transformed values, which Jesus advocated. The fact that Jesus lived 2,000 years ago and the end of the age has not arrived does not mean that the end of the age will not come. Although the historical Jesus might have been sur- prised that it is taking longer than he expected, the end of the age will ultimately come. Our modern scientific cosmology is one reason why we can say this with confidence: we now know that creation was not 10,000 years ago, but instead 15 billion years ago; and, just as we know our star is halfway through its life, we know that the end of the age will occur before our sun enters the "red giant phase" in 5 billion years' time. Jesus did not know all this scientific detail because communication in the first cen- tury required Jesus to assume a first-century cosmology.

Once again, we return to a crucial point that has been made repeatedly in this book. The disclosure of God must be local. God must communicate to a people in a way that will be understood. So it is with Jesus. It is undoubtedly the case that part of the self-understanding of Jesus is that he was an apocalyptic prophet working with a first-century cosmology. Jesus was understood by his contemporaries because he shared their cosmology and lived within a prophetic tradition that they recognized. This apocalyptic strand can be affirmed by contemporary Christians. Although we do need to disentangle the first-century cosmology, we continue to affirm the call of Jesus for transformed living by a different set of values.

Furthermore, we need to "transform" this picture of Jesus. The picture of Jesus emerging from Bart Ehrman's writings is incom- plete because it does not take into account the response that Jesus's preaching provoked. One unmistakable piece of data is that Jesus provoked in the monotheistic Jews around him such a sense of awe that they found themselves worshipping him.

It is worth remembering when we read the New Testament that the earliest sections are the letters of Paul. They come before the Gospel stories. The apocalyptic strand is still very much there: Paul clearly expected the world to end during his lifetime (see 1 Thessalonians 4: 13–18). However, there is another aspect which is equally, if not more, dominant: this is the Jesus who is being worshipped and adored as God.

We have Larry Hurtado to thank for a major study on "devotion to Jesus in earliest Christianity." As one reads the New Testament, the affirmation "Jesus is Lord" pulsates throughout the text. So many passages are a celebration of Jesus (see, for example, Colossians 1: 15–20, Acts 2: 36, and Philippians 2: 1–11). Hurtado shows that this devotion to Jesus did not emerge gradually but exploded on to the scene. Hurtado writes:

> Christians were proclaiming and worshipping Jesus, indeed, living and dying for his sake, well before the doctrinal/creedal developments of the second century . . . Moreover, devotion to Jesus as divine erupted suddenly and quickly, not gradually and late, among first-century circles of followers. More specifically, the origins lie in Jewish Christian circles of the earliest years.[10]

The sudden eruption, coupled with its home amongst Jewish monotheism, is clear evidence of the remarkable impact that the totality of Jesus's life, death, and resurrection had on the first Christians. Here we have Jews who, at considerable personal cost, believe in one God yet want to pray to and worship Jesus.

The point is that we do not simply have a Jewish prophet who preached the imminent end of the world. We also have a life that inspired followers to worship him. The clarity of expectation, the celebration of love, and the commitment to the outcast were all witness of a religiously significant leader that subsequent generations felt was worthy of worship.

The question now becomes this: should we trust those close to Jesus who insist that they have encountered a life worthy of worship? These initial Jewish followers are committed monotheists. They know how important it is to worship God and God alone. They are also making a decision that, for almost all the disciples, would cost them their lives. It was a "literal cross" which was taken up and carried. And there is, in my view, sufficient evidence pulsating through the New Testament of the transforming and demanding life of Jesus that helps us understand why the early Christians believed they were in the presence of God.

It was the act of worshipping Jesus that created the process culminating in the doctrines of the Trinity and Incarnation. The act of worshipping a life meant that the life must be God Incarnate; and if God is present in a life, then God must also – at the same time – be operating in different ways elsewhere (God was also sustaining the universe at the same time as God was in Christ dying on the cross). The doctrines of the Incarnation and Trinity are part of the logic of the worship of Jesus.

Naturally, the development of these doctrines took centuries. One would worry if they arrived at these complex formulations in haste. Although it is true that political and social factors also played their part (the Emperor Constantine did have an interest in a peaceful empire), this does not exclude the possibility that truth is being discovered. Political and social factors are part of the story of science, but science is still true.

So why do we trust the revelation of God in the life, death, and resurrection of Jesus? We do so because we trust the witness of Scripture that here was a life worthy of worship. And, for me, there are sufficient reasons in Scripture to show how those close to Jesus could see that this life was worthy of worship. In addition, we believe that this life is resurrected and still available to us through the Church and in the Sacrament. So we are all being invited to fall in love with Jesus and acknowledge that he is worthy of worship.

The challenge for the early Church was to explain how a life can be a revelation of God. Muslims and Jews understand entirely how a text can be the "Word of God," but a life is more puzzling. However, Jewish theology and Islamic theology did face the same question as Christians. What precisely is the relationship of the Word of God in the text with the Creator of the World? And the dominant answer in both traditions recognizes that the Word of God must be eternal and must have pre-existed creation. They both argue that anything that is part of God (and surely God's words must be part of God) cannot be changing and contingent, but must in some sense be part of God's own eternal existence.

Christians found themselves thinking in a similar way. We inherit from Judaism a conviction that God is the Father of everything. The image of father captures the transcendent source of all being – the creatorial aspect of God. Yet, in the life of Jesus, these monotheist Jews found themselves wanting to bow the knee. They saw in the life of Jesus a complete and definitive disclosure of what God is like.

It was the author of John's Gospel who saw what was going on. In the powerful prologue, the author explains:

> In the beginning was the Word and the Word was with God, and the Word was God. He was in the beginning with God; all things were made through him, and without him was not anything made that was made. . . . And the Word became flesh and dwelt among us, full of grace and truth; we have beheld his glory, glory as of the only Son from the Father. (John 1: 1, 2, 14)

Where the Father is an image for the aspect of God which creates, the Son is the image for the Eternal Word. Words are the expression of thoughts – they reveal us to others. So the author of John, chapter 1, is claiming that Jesus is the very expression of God – the revelation of God to humanity. The Eternal Word (the divine Wisdom – to pick up on another important image from Proverbs) made flesh.

So Christians found themselves talking about the Creator God (the Father) and the Eternal Word made flesh (the Son – Jesus). The next stage is how do these past events (Creation and Incarnation) relate to the present. The answer was found in Acts 2 – God sent the Holy Spirit (the aspect of God that makes God continually present) to be with us. The logic of worshipping a life had forced the Church to talk about the activity of God in three distinct ways. So the doctrine of the Trinity had been discovered.

Each member of the Trinity is involved in the work of the other two. Christians talked of the Son also being involved in creation – because through creation we can discern something of the nature of God. And, insofar as creation shows us something about God (i.e., it is revelatory), then the Son is at work in creation. Given that we can see in the present the fact of God at work in the miracles of creation, then the Holy Spirit is also at work in creation. So the work of the Father involves both the Son and the Holy Spirit.

So the next question is: how do we know what God is like? The Christian answer is that the Eternal Word of God completely interpenetrated the human life of Jesus so that when we look at the life, death, and resurrection of Jesus, we can see what God is like. The Word of God for Christians is a life.

It is precisely because the Word of God, in Christianity, is not a text but a life that we find ourselves encountering an adaptable Word. Of course, there is an important connection between the Word and the text of Scripture. For after all, it is the Bible that tells us about the Word, which is Jesus. Karl Barth is very helpful at this point. In Volume 1, Part 2, he explores at some length precisely what it means to call the Bible the Word of God. Barth explains:

> God is not an attribute of something else, even if this something else is the Bible. God is the Subject, God is Lord. He is Lord even over the Bible and in the Bible. The statement that the Bible is the Word of God cannot therefore say that the Word of God is tied to the Bible. On the contrary, what it must say is that Bible is tied to the Word of God. . . . If the Church lives by the Bible because it is the Word of God, that means that it lives by the fact that Christ is revealed in the Bible by the work of the Holy Spirit.[11]

For Karl Barth, the primary disclosure of God is the Word of God which is the life, death, and resurrection of Jesus of Nazareth. For Barth, the Bible becomes the Word as it witnesses to the Word, which is Jesus. And the manner in which this occurs is also determined by the Word of God Himself. Barth writes:

> As to when, where and how the Bible shows itself to us in this event as the Word of God, we do not decide, but the Word of God Himself decides, at different times in the Church and with different men confirming and renewing the event of instituting and inspiring the prophets and apostles to be His witnesses and servants, so that in their written word they again live before us, not as men who once spoke in Jerusalem and Samaria, to the Romans and Corinthians, but as men who in all the concreteness of their own situation and action speak to us here and now.[12]

For Barth, there is a Trinitarian dynamic at work between the Word of God, which is Jesus, and the Bible, as the Word of God. The Bible through the agency of the Holy Spirit can become an immediate text, confronting a particular moment, with the disclosure of God, which is the Eternal Word. With this emphasis on the primary Word is the Eternal Word, which completely interpenetrates the life of Jesus of Nazareth, and we can see that our primary obligation is to read a life – a life, which was very enigmatic.

Our definitive disclosure of what God is like shows us a poor young man from Nazareth who took enormous risks as he reached out to include the marginalized – especially women, the poor, and the reviled. He found himself a victim of power – finally dying as a common criminal at the hands of the occupying power. Yet, remarkably, the movement he birthed believed that death was not able to hold him. Reports of his resurrection started to circulate and so the Church was born.

So what do we know about God? We know that God is on the side of those who are least fortunate. We know that the love of God is willing to go to any length for the sake of humanity. We know that in our moments of despair, God promises to create hope. We know that we should treat this life as authoritative. We should imitate the "words and deeds" of Jesus of Nazareth.

Now our obligation as Christians is to recognize the authority of this life in guiding our witness today. This obligation extends to our interpretation of the rest of the Bible. If the Bible is interpreted in such a way as to contradict what we "read" from the life, death, and resurrection of the Eternal Word, then we have an obligation to revisit the text of the Bible. Although slavery is instituted in Leviticus and condoned in 1 Timothy, the legitimacy of slavery is clearly incompatible with the disclosure of God in the life, death, and resurrection of Jesus.

Reading the Qur'an can be difficult, but reading a life is harder.[13] So Christians are, right from the outset, bound to have to live with a pluralism of positions. Although the slavetraders are outside the zone of acceptable pluralism, there exists a multitude of positions with which the life of Jesus might be compatible. The areas of debate include the following: gratuitous war is clearly unacceptable, but the use of force to create a just peace might be acceptable; exploitative capitalism is clearly wrong, but the use of the profit motive to create an effective system of resource allocation might be acceptable; and life should not be created to be destroyed, but the cultivation of stem cells for the advancement of medical techniques that heal genetic diseases might be appropriate. Reading a life does have a major advantage over a text. It permits significant flexibility over time. We are imitating the "words and deeds" of Jesus. This exercise starts in the New Testament and shows how the Church struggles to arrive at the appropriate inclusive position over the Gentiles and the Jewish Law. And so it continues with Augustine and Aquinas.

The movement for Christian thought is to constantly move, to and fro, from the life, death, and resurrection of Jesus of Nazareth (as it flows through the sacraments and life of the Church) to the particularities of each situation. With the Spirit of God constantly making the Eternal Word present to each situation, we can and should allow our faith to engage with each situation, making use of all the resources available to us. The resources flow from our conviction of the threefold nature of God: a Creator who creates every single life and loves each particular life and seeks to disclose truth to those lives; a revealer and redeemer who discloses the nature of God (thereby providing a definitive norm) and also redeems all people; and a Spirit who is constantly making God present and allowing us to see God in new and different ways. These core convictions are responsible for a theology that is constantly engaging and changing. It might be ironic: but to be orthodox one should be open.

Now, the work of understanding Christian doctrine isn't easy, but a bright person like Richard Dawkins should be able to understand the summary above. It was the theologian Mike Higton who pointed out that one of the strangest aspects of Dawkin's entire project (and, with Dawkins, one can include Hitchens and Harris) is the complete lack of effort to even try to understand the internal logic and grammar of the Christian faith. Dawkins complains that it is all too difficult (and quotes with approval various postings from the Internet). So Dawkins writes, "most of us happily disavow fairies, astrology and the Flying Spaghetti Monster, without first immersing ourselves in books of Pastafarian theology etc."[14] And, by drawing the analogy between fairies and theism, with one stroke he reveals his ignorance. The narrative outlined in this chapter might be mistaken, but it captured the imagination of a third of the world's population because of its elegance and coherence, not despite it. As it happens, there are plenty of atheists who study theology and, of course, in so doing can make the case for atheism more effectively. Higton writes:

> Like believers in other religious traditions, Christians give certain kinds of reasons for what they say and do; they make certain kinds of proposals about what follows from what they say and do; they engage in certain kinds of arguments; they refer to certain kinds of norms. And because that is so, someone studying a theology course can investigate the emergence and current state of such patterns and practices of Christian reflection (drawing upon historical and ethnographic techniques in doing so) – and I do not think Dawkins would deny that – but she can go further, and spend time seeing where these patterns and practices might lead, or how they might be made more internally consistent, or how they might contain resources for responding to certain problems and challenges. The possibility of Christian theology as an academic discipline will rest, for the atheist student, upon the existence of the patterns, practices, resources, problems, and challenges; it need not rest upon the truth of Christianity's central claims.[15]

There is an internal logic to Christianity: it is not just a matter of words piled up on more words. And the reluctance of our atheist trio to do the hard work of understanding that logic undermines their project. Higton concludes this thoughtful article in the following way:

> He [i.e., Dawkins] simply does not take his own task seriously enough. If he were seriously interested in advancing atheism, seriously interested in taking the battle to the enemy's gate, seriously interested in convincing his more cogent opponents by argument (rather than settling for turning the heads of waverers with fireworks), he too would need to concern himself with overcoming inadequate and deluded accounts of the God hypothesis. If Richard Dawkins is serious about atheism, he really ought to be studying theology.[16]

At this point Dawkins is guilty of a basic sin of the academy. He wrote a book on a subject about which he knew very little: he set himself up as an authority on atheism, but never worked hard to understand the grammar of theism. In so doing, Dawkins betrayed the traditions of the university at which he works.

Implications

Returning to the project of explaining the internal logic of Christianity, it is worth appreciating the ways in which the doctrines of the Trinity and Incarnation overcome key challenges facing belief. The central religious problem is epistemological (which means – how do we know). So how do we know what God is like? How do we know which religion is right? Here we are small creatures in a vast solar system trying to work out what ultimate reality is like. How can we know when we have the right answers?

These questions are so obvious. Yet these questions are so difficult to answer. Ever since the European Enlightenment, people in the West have flirted with relativism or agnosticism. Relativism is attractive for some due to the long-standing argument that, given there is no way of knowing which religion is true, we should recognize the validity of all. Agnosticism becomes attractive because the range of different metaphysical answers suggests to some that there is no way of knowing the ultimate answers.

To avoid the twin challenges of relativism and agnosticism, all the faith traditions of the world respond in a similar way: we need to trust that somewhere there is a definitive disclosure of God. We need to trust a revelation of the transcendent. If we are going to guess what God is like, then agnosticism makes perfect sense. However, if we are going to make any sort of claim for knowledge, then we must trust that the gap between humanity and God has been bridged by God's initiative. As we have seen, for Jews, God's definitive disclosure is found in the Torah; for Muslims, it is in the Qur'an. Christians are in this respect no different. We also trust a revelation.

However, as we have seen, the location of this revelation is interesting. For Judaism and Islam, it is a text that is central. For

Christians, it is not a text but a life. Granted all knowledge of the past depends on texts (so a text, namely the Bible, becomes very important), but still the location of revelation is the life, death, and resurrection of Jesus of Nazareth. It is interesting when you look at our Creeds. Almost two thirds of the Apostles' Creed and perhaps just over half of the Nicene Creed focus on the telling of a narrative – they describe the life, death, and resurrection of Jesus. They talk about a person who came from heaven, was born of the Virgin Mary, was crucified under Pontius Pilate, rose again from the dead, and then ascended back into heaven. This narrative is the focus of the Creed. It is interesting how inadequate the Creed looks from the perspective of certain evangelical and fundamentalist traditions: it is not surprising that their "Statements of Faith" add a certain view of the Bible and the Atonement and, of course, today the importance of traditional marriage. In contrast the Nicene Creed keeps it simple: it is belief in God, belief in the Trinity, and a deep commitment to the life, death, and resurrection of Jesus of Nazareth.

The two key and distinctive doctrines of Christianity are the doctrines of the Trinity and the Incarnation. Both of these doctrines are attempting to make sense of Jesus – one within the life of God and the other as a human. In so doing, they explain what God is like. They give us a sense about the nature and being of the creator God.

So, for Dawkins, the edifice he needs to undermine to make his case for atheism effectively is the total edifice of a revealing God. This is a God who explains the mysteries of the mathematics of the universe; this is a God who is putting pressure on humanity, which most of the time we only appreciate partially. This is a God that Christians claim has definitely revealed the complexity of God in a person – in a life. The account provided of the Christian faith does not depend on an inerrant Scripture (the claim that the Bible is without error in any respect). This account builds on the insights of biologists and physicists. And this approach is one that is true to the best principles of Catholic Anglicanism.

7

Islam

Pity the moderate Muslims. They share the general post-9/11 anxiety about climbing on a plane; after all, they don't want the plane to blow up. They have to cope with the hurt and pain caused by the tragic and wicked behavior of co-religionists who committed crimes of terror. Then they have to handle the harassment: if you have a slightly darker skin or wear a *hijab*, you need to add plenty of extra time to your journey. And, finally, to top it all, one finds countless people who should know better reading Sam Harris and Christopher Hitchens, who take enormous pleasure in denigrating the Islamic faith and its followers.

One obvious question: why are these atheist writers getting so much attention now? And part of the answer is their fear of Islam. For secularists in Europe, there is a pervasive sense that religion does not matter any more. Churches are empty; and religion feels like a fringe activity. However, September 11 was a sudden wake-up call: suddenly they were reminded that most people in the world are religious and some take their religion very seriously. In much the same way, the controversy over the *fatwa* issued against Salman Rushdie created a semi-hysterical response in the 1980s; September 11 has birthed an entire volume.

There are differences between our three authors at this point. Harris is the worst; he makes Islamaphobia a central part of his message. Hitchens comes second; to his credit (perhaps), he recognizes that the bad aspects of Islam are also found in Christianity and Judaism (in fact, for Hitchens, there are no good religious traditions). And, for Dawkins, Islam is an illustration of the strange and bizarre behavior of religious people. It is interesting to note how both Harris and Hitchens supported the American war in Iraq, primarily as a result of their deep prejudice against Islam. As Tina Beattie points out:

> Hitchens remains unrepentant over his support for American and British interventions in Iraq. . . . Harris stands out as someone who makes no attempt at all to mask his contempt not only for radical Islamism but for Muslims in general, and who is willing to justify any violence, however extreme to fight the threat they represent.[1]

In a bizarre passage, Sam Harris decides to spend five pages listing all references to violence in the Qur'an.[2] We have already looked at the interesting way that the commandment to commit genocide in Deuteronomy 7 is immediately accompanied with a commandment not to intermarry. Religious texts need to be handled with care. And the exercise of just providing "proof-text" examples of violence in the Qur'an is as eccentric as declaring that Christians should be kosher because of Acts 15: 20, where, it is written, "but we should write to them to abstain only from things polluted by idols and from fornication and from whatever has been strangled and from blood" (NRSV). And the basic academic skills of locating the text in context (both within the book and within its historic setting and purpose) disappear. It also will not do to retort that there are plenty of Muslims and Christians who simply "proof text." First, the numbers who do this are fewer than Harris appreciates. But, second, one does not engage with a tradition by taking the worst representatives. The conversation should always take place with the finest representatives of a tradition. In politics, one struggles with Fredrick Hayek and his *Road to Serfdom* rather than Sean Hannity and his *Let Freedom Reign*. In philosophy, one engages with Immanuel Kant and the *Critique of Pure Reason* rather than Eric Cantona's *The Complete Cantona*.[3] It is of course easier to target those who are less sensitive to the complexities of their tradition, but it is not right. So let us attempt to understand the tradition a little more carefully.

Background on Islam

Muhammad was born into a challenging setting in 570 CE in what is today Saudi Arabia. Women were treated badly: infanticide of baby girls was a commonplace, and they had neither inheritance rights nor rights to divorce. Relationships between the tribes were often violent. And there was a lack of law and process. Into this setting, Muhammad witnessed to one God (rather than many gods). He insisted on the full equality of all women; he condemned unequivocally infanticide; and he provided the world with its first written constitution that established process and rights. In terms of a life, the fair observer cannot help but concede that he was a significant man.

It is easy to fixate on his marriage to Aisha at the age of nine, or to struggle with his decision to expel the Jewish tribe Banu Qaynuqa from Medina. Indeed, there are legitimate questions that can and should be asked. And these questions should not be underestimated. It is to the credit of so many Muslims that they are willing to engage in thoughtful conversation about these difficult questions.

However, one must look at a life in total – from prophet, administrator, military leader, and diplomat. Given the spheres that Muhammad moved in, it was a remarkable life.

The theology and worldview emerging from the Qur'an are equally outstanding. Islam is a way of life.[4] To be a Muslim is not simply to rationally assent to a belief system: instead it is a life-transforming, all-embracing way of behaving and living. This is done through the five pillars, which are described in the hadith.

Narrated Ibn 'Umar: Allah's Apostle said: Islam is based on [the following] five [principles]:
1. To testify that none has the right to be worshipped but Allah and Muhammad is Allah's Apostle.
2. To offer the [compulsory congregational] prayers dutifully and perfectly.
3. To pay Zakat [i.e., obligatory charity].
4. To perform Hajj [i.e., Pilgrimage to Mecca].
5. To observe fast during the month of Ramadan.[5]

These five pillars provide a rich framework for the human life. So, starting with prayer: it is incumbent upon all Muslims to pray five times a day – daybreak, noon, mid-afternoon, sunset (although not at the actual setting of the sun), and evening. Having undergone the ritual washing, anyone can pray, anywhere, provided the place is clean. Such washing is an appropriate sign of respect. The obligation to pray at least five times a day is the bare minimum. The idea here is that God is sensitive to our human fallibility: the ease with which a day can pass without even a thought for our Creator. So these five times are required: five opportunities to remember the God whom Muslims serve – his compassion, his mercy and his justice.

These five times should forge a chain linking together more and more moments of remembrance, so that ultimately God comes to dominate everything one thinks, does, and feels. Moving now to fasting: as prayer times break up the day and require the believer to remember the compassion of the Creator, so Ramadan plays the same role in the year. For one month, during the daylight hours, neither food nor drink should be taken. It is a month of fasting and celebration that helps give the year its rhythmic turning around the compassion of God. As prayer is to the day, and fasting is to the year, so the pilgrimage is to the life. Mecca is the holiest place in creation: it is the source of the Qur'anic revelations. It is required for Muslims, once in their lifetime, to make a pilgrimage for seven days to Mecca. Pilgrims must have earned sufficient funds to pay for the trip, ensured that they have provided enough to support their dependents, and then, with the endorsement of the community, will be sent to Mecca. Before entering Mecca, any jewelry is removed and clothes are exchanged for wraps (i.e., *ihram* – simple clothing), to ensure that pilgrims are now indistinguishable from each other. Visits are made to Safa and Marwah, and then to Arafat where Muhammad delivered his farewell sermon. At Mina they throw pebbles at a pillar representing Satan (symbolizing their rejection of evil) and make a sacrifice of a sheep or a goat (symbolizing their willingness to sacrifice their lives for God).

Central to the *hajj* is the cube-shaped stone building Ka'ba, which is located in the open court of the Grand Mosque. It is a copy of the original built by Abraham and Ishmael. Abraham is venerated because he was the first monotheist in the region; Ishmael – according to the tradition – is their ancestor. Around 2–3 million Muslims make the pilgrimage every year.

The last pillar is related to giving. Islam is an intensively practical religion. It is a community religion: those who have must provide for the full-time servants of Allah and the poor. It is a religious obligation – as important as prayer – to provide for those who find living difficult. The obligation is to give as much as you can spare which, according to most authorities, will be at least one-fortieth of one's annual wealth. Islam touches everything: it is a religion for both the spirit and the body.

This brief introduction to Islam should at least challenge the wicked caricature that one finds in the work of Sam Harris. For the vast majority of Muslims, this is their life. Granted there are some Muslims who are less observant (as with Christians, Jews, and every religion), yet for those who live this tradition to the full, there is a compelling beauty.

However, the questions remain: what about the suicide bombers? What about the terrorist threat from *jihadists*? It is to these questions that we turn next.

Terrorism

Let it be said loud and clear: to put on an explosive belt and walk into a restaurant is a deeply evil act. It involves the double sin of taking one's own life and the taking of innocent non-combatants. To create a culture which celebrates such actions is also wrong. To reward, support, and encourage such a culture is also wrong. And the vast majority of Muslims would agree with me.

Let me also say this loud and clear. Most Muslims are not terrorists. There is a small minority of Muslims who are sympathetic or involved in terrorism, but the majority is not.

One essential imperative in this debate is to allow for nuance. For example, the popular picture of a Muslim is someone from the Middle East. However, most Muslims are not Arabs. The most populated Islamic country is Indonesia (some 180 million Muslims), which combined with, say, India is a great deal more than the entire population of the Middle East.

It is very important to recognize that there is considerable variety in Islam, extending to forms of Islam that are deeply committed to non-violence. For example, there are some 9 million followers of Beduizzaman Said Nursi (1877–1960). Said Nursi, a Turkish thinker, taught that to resort to violence showed a lack of confidence in the beauty and truth of Islam to persuade others. In addition, the goal of Islam is to transform a human life so that the virtue of peace radiates through. An amount of 9 million followers makes it twice the population of Wales.[6] Unlike the famous Egyptian Brotherhood (one of the more militant, yet very small), this is, numerically, a significant group.

It is also important to recognize that the practice of suicide bombing is not peculiar to Islam. The West has been preoccupied with the story of "virgins" awaiting the martyrs in paradise. Then this was disturbed by the phenomenon of female suicide bombers, which provoked a semi-patriarchal reaction – they (meaning the Muslims) even send their women to kill themselves and others. Lindsey O'Rourke, in a recent article analyzing the phenomenon of female suicide bombers, makes two very pertinent points. The first is that there is no single biography of a female suicide bomber – some are religious and others are secular. She writes:

> From the unmarried communists who first adopted suicide terrorism to expel Israeli troops from Lebanon in the 1980s, to the so-called Black Widows of Chechnya who commit suicide attacks after the combat deaths of their husbands, to the longtime adherents of the Liberation Tigers of Tamil Eelam separatist movement in Sri Lanka, the biographies of female suicide attackers reveal a wide variety of personal experiences and ideologies.[7]

The second point is that it is just factually false to blame Islam. O'Rourke writes:

> Blaming Islamic fundamentalism is also wrongheaded. More than 85 percent of female suicide terrorists since 1981 committed their attacks on behalf of secular organizations; many grew up in

Christian and Hindu families. Further, Islamist groups commonly discourage and only grudgingly accept female suicide attackers.[8]

It is extraordinary that writers such as Harris and Hitchens who pride themselves on "reason" and "research" never did the basic research on this phenomenon. Plenty of secularists (mainly influenced by the atheist philosophy of Marxism) had strapped on the explosive belt and gone to war. The whole picture is much more complicated.

However, let us concede that al-Qaeda is real enough. And this does require some analysis to understand what is going on here.

Al-Qaeda

The place to go for a good summary of the factors that created "radical Islam" is Greg Barton's delightful book *Jemaah Islamiyah*.[9] And the place to begin is Saudi Arabia.

The hijackers on September 11 were all from Saudi Arabia. And the form of Islam practiced in Saudi Arabia has been rightly implicated as a factor. Muhammad ibn Abd al-Wahhab – the reformer who shaped official state Islam in Saudi Arabia – argued for a form of Islam that rejected the accretions that had developed over centuries since the life of the Prophet. On one level, this was extremely innocent, and there is a lively literature both for and against Wahhabi Islam (or the term preferred by followers – Salafism). Yet, on another level, this created problems. The Islam practiced by most Muslims was now problematic; we had the seeds of a "cult" emerging inside the religion.[10] So, although in itself Wahhabi Islam can be benign, it created a potent and deadly mix when combined with the Muslim Brotherhood founded in Egypt.

The Muslim Brotherhood founded in 1928 by Hassan al-Barina was heavily shaped by Sayyid Qutb. Qutb was seen by many as a "martyr" (because he was killed by the Egyptian government). Due to his bad experience in America, Qutb argued that all human society was in a state analogous to Mecca before the arrival of the Prophet Muhammad (i.e., one of depravity and ignorance of all things divine, which is called *jahiliah* in Arabic).

Qutb writes, "At the time of the Prophet's call to Messengership, the moral level of Arabia was extremely low from every point of view. Only a few primitive tribal customs prevailed."[11] What was needed then, explains Qutb, was not a reform movement, but a transformation grounded in true belief in the One God. And Muhammad succeeded in bringing about this transformation. So Qutb writes:

> All this was possible because those who established this religion in the form of a state, a system and laws and regulations had first established it in their hearts and lives in the form of faith, character, worship and human relationships. They had been promised only one thing for the establishment of this religion – not victory or power, not even that this religion would be established by their hands, not related to anything of this world – one promise, that of the Garden. That was the only promise given to them for all their striving, for all the trials which they had endured, for their steadfastness in the face of the opposition of the forces of Jahiliyyah to that call, "There is no deity except God," which is abhorrent to those who are in power in any age and place.[12]

Having established the imperative of radical struggle against the forces of unbelief in the time of the Prophet, Qutb argues that we live in a comparable time now, which needs comparable radical struggle. He attacks the view that Islam can be practiced by individuals without an Islamic state. He insists that Islam was founded as a project which "included the whole of life."[13] He disagrees strongly that *jihad* is primarily about "self-defense." Those who talk like this, explains Qutb, are "defeated by the present difficult conditions and by the attacks of the treacherous orientalists on the Islamic jihad."[14] So this is a call for violent struggle and overthrow of the regimes that are depraved. Struggle, argued Qutb, is needed to create a culture honoring God.

The third ingredient was facilitated by the West. Greg Barton explains:

> The twentieth century is not lacking in instances of short-sighted folly in the foreign policy of western nations. High on the list of "great mistakes of our age" would have to be the decision to work

with the Pakistan Inter-Services Intelligence directorate (ISI) and Saudi Arabia's foreign intelligence service, the euphemistically named Foreign Liaison Office, in sponsoring *mujahidin* to fight against the Soviets in Afghanistan.[15]

So, in what must go down as the single biggest mistake of the latter part of the twentieth century, America decided to solicit the support of these *jihadists* in Afghanistan against the Russian occupation. If this hadn't happened, then these groups in the Middle East would have probably functioned much like the English and American Marxist revolutionaries in the 1920s and 1930s – lots of noise, plenty of meetings, but very little action. Barton explains how three factors (namely, "the radicalizing experience of fighting on the battlefields of Afghanistan as *mujahidin*, the natural bonding that comes from being brothers-in-arms, and the rich experience of studying in terrorism colleges along both sides of the Afghanistan-Pakistan border as God's vanguard proven in battle") created "class after class of 'Afghan alumni' ready to return home and continue the struggle."[16] In other words, Afghanistan turned hundreds of *jihadists* into seasoned soldiers. An army had been created.

The combination of a Wahhabi framework, Qutb's analysis, and of course field experience in Afghanistan created the terror network known as al-Qaeda. Everything was in place. Deeply disturbed by the presence of American troops in Saudia Arabia and believing the West is corrupt and blasphemous, war was declared. The weapon was the suicide bomber. The targets were symbols of power. The objective was death and mayhem.

Greg Barton has argued that al-Qaeda needed all three factors to emerge as a significant threat to the West. Although al-Qaeda has a religious vision, the conditions that enabled it to organize the September 11 attacks extend far beyond religion. In particular it needed the Afghanistan field experience, which the West provided.

The vision of a religion as sketched by those on the margins should not be taken as indicative of the religion as a whole. A secularist would resent being constantly linked to Stalin's persecution of the Russian people. So a Muslim is entitled to resent the constant association with al-Qaeda. This is prejudice pure and simple – a prejudice that permeates the work of our atheist trio.

Islam and the Revealing God

One question remains for consideration in this chapter. This chapter on Islam is the culmination of a section that explored the "revealing God" as seen through indigenous traditions, Judaism, Christianity, and Islam. Although it has been necessary to look at Islam and terrorism due to the charges made by Harris, Hitchens, and Dawkins, this would be very unfair to this remarkable tradition if the chapter finished on that point.

As a Christian, I believe that the Eternal Word has been disclosed in the person of Jesus of Nazareth. And, from the New Testament, one learns about a God who loves all humanity and is constantly reaching out to all humanity. As Paul explains in Romans 9–11, God is continuing to be in relationship with the Jewish people. Therefore, we have every reason to believe that God is deep in conversation with those who are Muslims. The elegance of the five pillars and the power of their practice are ample evidence of the presence of the Spirit of God in Islam.

So what am I doing here? First, where Christians and Muslims agree, there is clear evidence that God Almighty is getting through to humanity. But, second, I am accounting for the manifest goodness in Islam in terms that are internal to the Christian tradition. I do believe it is the Triune God that engages Muslims. Naturally, Muslims would contest this and have their own internal explanation for Christians. They would insist that Christians have a partial revelation (which we have distorted), but nevertheless are "people of the book." This work of providing internal explanations for disagreements is common across much intellectual inquiry: Dawkins accounts for religion as a meme; a Marxist accounts for a capitalist using the category of class; and a Muslim accounts for Christianity as a movement that had a partial revelation of the truth that God finally clarified in the Qur'an.

How do we know which religion is correct? The answer to this is that we recognize our rootedness, continue the conversation, and work hard to discern the religious account that is most plausible, most coherent, and has the greater explanatory power. This is hard work, but not impossible. As things stand, I am making a claim for a certain strand of Christianity; naturally, my Muslim friends would disagree. And so we are both forced into a divinely intended conversation to discern where the truth lies.

8

Suffering, Providence, and Horrid Religious People

The case against our atheists is slowly taking shape. Thus far, I have argued that the implications of their atheism are not faced: they have not read or engaged with their atheist critics (such as Nietzsche and his successors) who believe that a world without God is much more dramatic than they assume. Such categories as "truth" and "moral," which Dawkins et al. continue to use effortlessly, were formed in a religious environment and need radical reinterpretation if the categories are going to survive. This constant attack by our atheist trio on the indoctrination of children demonstrates a basic misunderstanding of what the gift of faith involves. "Seeing God" requires the training of our spiritual sense. In the same way that parents encourage a child to learn a musical instrument or to learn a language, so they should encourage the cultivation of the "spiritual sense." There are good reasons to believe that the human sense of spirituality is tapping into an objective reality. The challenge of making sense of morality and great art strongly suggests such a reality. But the best argument is the one emerging from modern physics. We have to account for the remarkable data around the various factors that enabled life to emerge in this universe. Dawkins opts for the multiverse theory, which has a range of conceptual and scientific problems. The simpler explanation is the God hypothesis.

Given this, we started a journey. Knowledge of any God is going to depend on revelation. Dawkins et al. have lots of fun looking at this or that text in the Hebrew Bible, the New Testament, and the Qur'an. And once again they betray a lack of real engagement with the text. I offered an account of how God puts pressure on humanity, initially in the indigenous traditions, and later in the written traditions of Judaism, Christianity, and Islam. On the way, I sketched an account of the doctrines of the Trinity and the Incarnation, defending both the coherence and plausibility of such doctrines. In our discussion of Islam, we confronted the manifest Islamaphobia that is part of this sudden resurgence of atheism.

Our response to atheism is nearly complete. However, two more areas need sustained attention. The first is to extend our account of the Christian faith (although much that is written might provoke the assent of some Jews and Muslims) to the areas of providence, suffering, and ethics. The second is to consider the sociological data. Is it the case that religion is really on the way out? Is Dawkins right to claim that scientists are embarrassed by people of faith? Is this trinity of books really an illustration of a movement in that direction?

So it is to the first of these two areas that we turn next.

Providence and Suffering

Every night on the television, there are countless stories of people hurting. Every human life is touched by suffering and pain. Every person of faith has had moments of acute struggle as he or she thinks through the "why" question. Why is it that a God of goodness and love allows evil and suffering?

Christians recognize that there is no answer sufficient to explain the horrendous pain of the Holocaust or the tragedy of a child being abducted, tortured, and raped. At moments such as these Natalie and Fred sit next to each other – weeping, perhaps holding each other's hands.

The Bible is interesting in this respect. There is no "theoretical explanation" for suffering and pain and yet the text pulsates with the issue. Every pain documents the problem. Sometimes it is pain caused by humanity and, at other moments, pain caused by natural disasters. The Psalms have countless expressions of humanity crying out in anguish against the injustice of it all; and the book of Job is a masterpiece – a reflection on why "good people suffer." Ultimately, for a Christian, there is a sense in which the only adequate response is Good Friday. It is the moment when Christians sit and meditate on the first-century equivalent of the "electric chair" and recognize that God Almighty suffered and died. Whatever the cosmic reason is for suffering and pain, the fact that God suffered is part of the Christian response.

In *Understanding Christian Doctrine*, I argued that there is a sense that all Christian theology is part of the response to suffering and evil. The Fall (which we have already examined) explains the propensity of humanity to inflict so much suffering and pain; the good news of redemption is the miracle that God is creating the possibility of a human life living for the purposes of love rather egotism; and the hope beyond the grave is the promise of redemption for all life forms made possible by the miracle of resurrection.

However, I entirely understand how inadequate this all sounds for our atheist trio. Harris would object that a response at the level of heart and feeling is insufficient; there is a logical problem that needs solving here. How and why does an omnipotent and loving God allow a Holocaust or the rape of a child?

Now, at this point, we return to one of the ironic themes of this book. The modern scientific account of reality is perhaps helping us to see options that previously were not available. New models of the universe are emerging that are helping us to see things differently.

Divine action

Keith Ward in *Divine Action* finds the game of dice an interesting way into the issues of suffering and providence. When one plays dice, one needs the game to be random (otherwise there is no game), yet every single time one has a turn one desperately wants to throw a six.[1] In addition, the game itself is governed by certain basic laws of mechanics, yet the game does not just continue by itself. An external agent in terms of a player is needed to keep the game going. Even though one can reduce the game to the math of mechanics, it is not a complete explanation for what is going on.[2]

So let us unpack this game of dice image. God had certain macro intentions in creating this world (or to use the language of Aquinas – God's antecedent willing), but also has certain micro desires within the world (i.e., the consequent willing). God created a universe in which life with the capacity for freedom could emerge. This was God's antecedent willing. However, once these lives are operating in the world, God is constantly calling us to exercise our freedom for love and good (the consequent willing). However, God cannot simply compel us to behave in certain ways because that would override the antecedent willing. In the same way, even though we are desperate for a six to win a certain game of dice, we wouldn't want the game to cease being random. Although God desires a world where human beings live in peace with each other, God also does not constantly destroy our freedom to bring that state about.

The picture from modern physics seems to support this picture of divine action. Physics has changed dramatically from the mechanism universe advocated by Newton and celebrated by Laplace. Although we should be careful not to overstate the picture emerging from the discoveries in quantum physics, it does open up possibilities for divine action. Keith Ward summarizes:

> [S]ince the development of quantum theory in this century it has become most plausible to see the physical world as a set of emergent, flexible and open systems, and Newtonian mechanics as "no more than an approximation to a more supple reality". In this sense, the material world is open to a purposive shaping of the flexible cosmos of becoming – it is open . . . When the universe is most naturally seen as an open and emergent system, a much more positive space has been cleared for a creative dimension either to emerge within this reality, or, as the theist would believe, to direct its processes as their root.[3]

Thanks to quantum mechanics, the concepts of human free will (and the related concept of divine agency) are no longer manifestly unscientific. As Immanuel Kant discovered, the Newtonian universe left no room for human free will. For, in Newton's universe, the next segment of the world was "caused" by the prior segment, and, as Laplace found, the concepts of innovation just didn't seem to make scientific sense. So the presumption emerged: innovation is really an allusion.

Now, however, we are talking about an "open" and "emergent" universe. At the quantum level, we know this is true. There are in the world of atoms actions that are uncaused. So new models of the universe are emerging: ones in which human agency can make some sense because a decision by a human mind is somehow part of this "uncaused" quantum world.

If human agency is making some sense, then perhaps divine agency can be analogous. It looks as if God can use similar avenues within the universe to bring about certain desired ends. Due to God's antecedent willing, God is – until the eschaton (end of the world) – going to work within the constraints of the creation. So God is not going to suddenly make all missiles into candyfloss by a single divine action; but God is going to answer prayers for healing and will work to deepen the desire for love inside an individual's human soul.

The picture here is this: the entire universe is part of the life of God. God as spirit is able to embrace everything that is. God has allowed the processes of the Big Bang and the gradual expansion of the universe to generate a planet with the capacity to shape life. In these processes, God has been constantly at work to ensure certain ends are realized. As creatures emerged with the capacity of decision and freedom, God is now seeking our cooperation in the cosmic project of "love." Sometimes we cooperate; however, sometimes we choose to thwart.

The suffering caused by earthquakes, hurricanes, and other natural disasters are often part of the necessary constraints and structure of the universe. To have a world without these aspects would require a very different world. The suffering we inflict on each other is a necessary part of the project of love. God cannot have creatures with the capacity to love, without also having the capacity for hate and violence.

In this picture, God is constantly seeking to inspire us to cooperate with this love project. And as we exercise decisions and change the world, so God is exercising decisions and changing the world as well. The idea of prayer involves this work of cooperation with God. Keith Ward challenges a popular misconception about prayer. Surely, a person might object, God will do what is best regardless of our prayers? Ward responses to this objection by writing:

> But this neglects the co-operative nature of the Divine action. God cannot heal all suffering, without destroying the structure of this world entirely. But part of that structure is that people can freely help or harm one another. They can increase or decrease suffering by their actions. As they relate to God, they can increase or decrease the possibilities of the Divine governance of things. Sin closes off possibilities of Divine action; whereas obedient love opens up new channels for Divine action. When we show such love by praying for others, we may open up channels of healing that God can use; creatures and creator can cooperate in making the world more transparent to Divine influence.[4]

When we pray, we are creating space for God to act. We are opening up channels – perhaps at the quantum level – for love to act and make a difference.

Now, given the interconnected nature of the universe, there is a constant battle between destructive human decisions and loving human decisions. And the matrix of interconnecting patterns is considerable. In many cases, the factors involved in the patterns are both a mixture of good and bad, tragic and heroic. So, for example, if Nelson Mandela had not been imprisoned (bad and tragic) then South Africa would not have had his inspired leadership to manage a nation as it moves from an oppressive apartheid regime to a democracy (good and heroic). The apartheid regime was upheld by many very determined white people, who were exercising their freedom for evil ends. Now the divine respect for human freedom makes it difficult for God to simply override the apartheid regime. And perhaps – and this is contentious, but it makes sense – God's capacity to predict the future means that God does not simply respond to the prayers of the African National Congress and liberate Nelson Mandela prior to the slow erosion of the apartheid regime. The matrix of factors in this pattern is deeply interwoven with bad and good constantly intersecting.

So let us stop talking about a God who is a remarkable magician and can conjure new situations where everything has changed; let us stop talking about a God who can prevent every evil effortlessly without affecting human freedom and decision. Let us instead see this universe for what it is. This is a universe where God is constantly seeking the cooperation of humans through prayer and through decisions for good to make the world different.

Given the complex intersecting of patterns, it is perfectly proper to talk about the request from a person, in a prayerful relationship with God, as being an important factor. The claim of Scripture is that sometimes God does allow a certain future to materialize precisely because we ask. In the same way as a friend might decide not to play a game of golf but go with another friend to a basketball game instead, so God allows a different future to emerge because we have asked. "[I]f the divine plan is to a large extent open, he may consent to realize a certain state just because it is requested. The making of the request is a new fact of the total situation to which God will respond. It is an additional factor of which he will take due account. If he does take account of it, this increases the degree to which a fully personal relationship can exist between creatures and God."[5] So we have a God who is constantly searching for the way forward, but does so recognizing the complex interlocking matrix of good and bad already in the world. In addition, one of those factors that God must take into account is the prayer of a person with whom God already has a deep relationship. Prayers take different forms: and those prayers already steeped in an understanding and commitment to the reality of God have a real capacity to create both space for God to act and to enable God to respond.

At this point, someone might object in the following way: why doesn't God just take the best possible option in any given situation? Surely an omniscient being (a being that knows everything that is logically possible for God to know) would always do this. The problem with this, explains Ward, is that there is no such thing as a "best option." There are many possible futures available at any moment in time, many of which are good. Granted some are bad (an act of murder for example), but whether I become a Dean of a Seminary or a Rector of a Church – both can be good. God has created a world where God can take our participation very seriously in the next segment of creation.

So to summarize this section of the chapter: how does God act? God acts by creating a universe that is genuinely open to both human agency and divine agency. Although the universe is predictable in so many ways, there is built in an openness that makes all the difference to the possibility of the exercise of free will and divine agency. Why does God allow suffering? God allows suffering because God could not have a universe of this type without the possibility of human agents being wicked and the structures of the universe inflicting enormous pain within the system.

This brief response to the tragedy of suffering within the world might seem insensitive. So once again we return to the text of Scripture. As noted at the start of this chapter, it is interesting that the Bible never provides an explanation for suffering. The book of Job is a remarkable text, which really struggles over the problem of evil and suffering, and concludes with the declaration that little human creatures can never know the mind of the Creator. So, although I have suggested that modern physics is providing an insight into why God allows suffering, I do recognize that the response of the Bible is different.

Dawkins alludes to the biblical response in passing. It is the cross. Dawkins notes how odd it is that a cross is hanging at the front of a church. Dawkins writes:

> It is, when you think about it, remarkable that a religion should adopt an instrument of torture and execution as its sacred symbol, often worn around the neck. Lenny Bruce rightly quipped that "If Jesus had been killed twenty years ago, Catholic school children would be wearing little electric chairs around their necks instead of crosses."[6]

And, although Richard Dawkins doesn't get it, this is precisely the point. For Christians, the primary response to the problem of suffering in creation is not an argument, but a person and an event. So we return to the point at which this chapter started: it is Jesus of Nazareth, who is believed to be the Incarnation of God, who hangs and dies on the cross. When we worship God, we worship a suffering God. We worship a God who has identified with the pain of all in creation.

For Christians, this means that when God decided to embark on this creatorial project, God knew that this would extract a significant price for the creator. It would cost. And, as we puzzle from our vantage point as to why God allows so much suffering in the creation, we are constantly reminded through worship of the participation of God in the processes, challenges, and suffering of being human.

Another important response to the reality of evil and suffering within the creation is the constant call to "live differently." A primary goal of the religious life is to live with love. So let us now turn to the problem of religion and ethics. Why are religious people often so unethical?

Religion and Ethics

Let us start by standing back. Why is anyone cruel or unkind? The Christian answer is "sin." Now sin is a complex notion. Sin is often an act of hubris – it is that act of denial of our dependence (on air, food, a world) and interdependence (on each other, on the environment). And, ultimately, we are dependent on the creator, who sustains and enables everything to be. Sin is therefore deeply irrational. It is absurd to imagine that we are not dependent, yet there are countless moments when we imagine we can strike out on our own.

The striking out on our own is almost always an act of selfishness. We assert an egotistical want or need and decide that our "interdependence" does not matter. So to take two illustrations of this – materialism and lust – we find the following. With materialism,we focus on an acquisition that we are sure will make all the difference and thereby deny the resource spent on that acquisition that was needed by someone else; and with "lust" (another old-fashioned word), the sexual desire so overwhelms us that we forget a promise to another and create havoc and damage as a result.

The Christian claim is that no human life is immune from the illusions of sin. All human lives are sinful. This is not simply true of individuals, but also religious organizations. The fact that a person is religious does not make them sinless. And religion (like all human activities) can be taken over by sin. In fact, good and bad are seen everywhere. In the same way that the game of soccer can become dominated by excessive salaries and crowd violence, so religion can be distorted into a damaging human practice.

Even science is a human activity that can be hijacked. Fritz Lenz (1887–1976) was a leading specialist of "racial hygiene" for the Nazis. With a specialization in eugenics, he was an advocate and practitioner of a variety of evil programs. He worked alongside Otmar Freiherr von Verschuer (1896–1969) who directed the program that worked on human subjects from Auschwitz. There is nothing that sin cannot touch. So Christians are not surprised to learn that Christian institutions often behave badly. We regret this reality, but we do not deny it. Although we wish it were different, we cannot evade this truth.

Christians should and do repent of a past that includes much ambiguity (to put it kindly) and wickedness (to put it more brutally). So Christians acknowledge that the crusades were wrong; the imaginative torture techniques involved in the Inquisition were evil; and the cleric from the city of Liverpool in the UK, who provided a learned justification of the slave trade, was deeply mistaken.

We can also acknowledge and repent of the ways in which religion becomes a part of a wider complex of factors that shape a situation. So, in the North of Ireland, there were religious dynamics at work. However, there were also other dynamics – political, social, and economic ones – at work. It is just not true to say that if one eliminated the religious difference then there would never have been a problem in the North of Ireland.

Now, granted that there are not very many atheists in history, it is true that religion has played a part in tragic situations more than atheism. However, in the twentieth century, perhaps the century when violence touched more lives than any other, atheists did appear on the scene. Christopher Hitchens spends his time claiming that all tyrants are really religious. In one of the weaker parts of his book, he credits religion with Stalin and Hitler – they show religious characteristics by being tyrants. Hitchens wants to try and win the argument by definition: religion implies tyranny, therefore any tyrant is a religious. This is a manifestly fallacious argument. And Stalin, just to take one prominent atheist of the twentieth century, would have resented the association with religion. Dawkins is wrong to assert that Stalin's atheism was not a factor in his brutality. He used a variety of tools – persecution, harassment, and murder – to minimize the Church. As Borden Painter reminds Dawkins: "That assertion ignores the historical record as recounted by major historians of modern European history. Stalin's government conducted savage persecutions of believers in the name of scientific atheism as policy, sponsoring the League of the Miltant Godless and frequently setting up museums of atheism in churches."[7]

Dawkins suspects that there are fewer atheists in prison. Again, given Dawkins has the advantage of atheists being in a distinct minority, this is probably true. Let us also concede that there are plenty of good atheists. Atheists can be found helping their neighbor, advocating for justice issues, and living the life of virtue. However, my worry is the connection between behavior and rationality.

This is a point that Dawkins might find interesting. As Nietzsche demonstrated, moral discourse without God is difficult to justify. So, although I am delighted that there are moral atheists, my fear is that they will start thinking and cease using moral categories. There is the very fundamental problem of justification. As we have already noted, one of the oldest question in the history of ideas is – why not be selfish? Or, to put it in such a way that acknowledges the Darwinian arguments for altruism – why not encourage others to be altruistic, yet be selfish when one can be undetected? The language of morality implies an external realm which is binding on human behavior. Without this external realm, the temptation of the rational egoist might become overwhelming for the atheist.

In a rational world, where the implications of atheism are faced, there is a real risk of atheism opting for rational egoism. Fortunately, most atheists are not rational. And these atheists continue to use concepts and language, formed in a religious culture, as part of their worldview. Dawkins is a good example of an irrational atheist. However, I am not sure whether the delightful, yet incoherent, humanism of Dawkins can survive. Ultimately, even atheists will end up thinking.

So, while empirically I am willing to concede that there are plenty of examples of religious people behaving very badly, rationally, the moral life does depend on the life of faith. And, fortunately, there are plenty of examples of moral people who work hard, serve others, and seek to live their faith with sincerity and love. Robin Gill's excellent study on *Churchgoing and Christian Ethics* does demonstrate that ultimately religious people do behave better than their non-churchgoing counterparts.

Persons of faith are on strong ground in the area of morals. I think the case can be made that, both in respect to behavior and justification, religious people are more ethical.

9

Religion and the Future

These fundamentalist atheists claim to be a persecuted minority (they alone can see the truth and have the courage to stand up for it) and at the same time they claim that they are the dominant trend of the future (most scientists are atheists and lots of Americans are). We explore this contradiction. We discover in this chapter that the secularization thesis is increasingly rejected by social sciences. Religion is here to stay.

The Dominant Trend: Their Books are Selling

Primarily, our authors are sympathetic to the secularization thesis. However, a more trivial reason is the popularity of their books. At this point, they are guilty of a *fallacy of excessive royalty income*. And it is one that many authors of bestsellers commit. It is true that Harris, Hitchens, and Dawkins have written books that many people have appreciated. And some of these people have written letters and sent emails to the authors, expressing their appreciation. So Richard Dawkins starts the paperback edition with the words: *"The God Delusion* in the hardback edition was widely described as the surprise bestseller of 2006. It was warmly received by the great majority of those who sent in their personal reviews to Amazon (more than 1000 at the time of writing)."[1] Dawkins is imagining that the sales (and positive

Amazon reviews) are indicative of a movement that will make a difference – a movement that he hopes will be called the "Brights"![2] So the "successful book sales means that we are the future" argument does need to be confronted explicitly. And what Dawkins needs to realize is that in a world of 6 billion people, success is very local.

A good example of this *fallacy of excessive royalty income* is the remarkable achievement of the Left Behind series. The Left Behind series sold more than 50,000,000 copies of the various books in the series on January 12, 2002.[3] Since then it is continuing to go from success to success; the translated editions are doing well – over a million copies of the books and tapes have been sold in twelve different languages.[4] *Publishers Weekly* announced that *Desecration* was the number one bestselling hardcover fiction title in 2001, displacing John Grisham who had previously held that slot over the seven previous years. These books are not simply read, but they are shared; they are studied; they are extensively discussed on the Internet. These books are preoccupying many Christians both in America and around the world.

For the benefit of Richard Dawkins, the amazing phenomenon is a fictional portrayal of the "end times." Grounded in a pre-millennial dispensationalist theology, it imagines a rapture (where millions of Christians mysteriously disappear) followed by a seven-year tribulation, which culminates in the Battle of Armageddon. Starting in the present, the first book starts with the night flight from Chicago to London, midway across the Atlantic, on a 747 jetliner. Stillness descends upon the cabin, which is then disturbed by first an elderly woman discovering that her husband is missing; only to be rapidly followed by many other passengers complaining that family members have disappeared. The only things left are the clothes (all neatly left in their seats). The mysterious disappearance of people on the aircraft is part of a worldwide spontaneous disappearance of millions of people. This is the "rapture" – the call of the Church out of the world to be saved from the judgment of God that will follow in the Tribulation. The first in the series was called *Left Behind*, rapidly followed by *Tribulation Force, Nicolae, Soul Harvest, Apollyon,*

Assassins, *The Indwelling*, *The Mark*, *Desecration*, *The Remnant*, *Armageddon*, and *Glorious Appearing*.

The authors behind this publishing phenomenon are Dr. Tim LaHaye and Jerry B. Jenkins. LaHaye is the Bible scholar. Equipped with his DMin from Western Theological Seminary, he has become a leading advocate of "pre-Trib" theory and founded the PreTrib Research Center. Even before the Left Behind Series, he was a prolific author, with *The Spirit-Controlled Temperament* being his best-known book. Although he is by no means the first to offer a fictional portrayal of the End Times, the Left Behind series was his idea. To deliver it, he teamed up with Jerry B. Jenkins. LaHaye provides the prophetic outline that Jenkins turns into a narrative. Prior to the Left Behind series, Jenkins was the ghost writer behind several biographies. His background is in Christian publishing: he was the editor of *Moody Magazine*. There is no doubt that this team is reaching the hearts and minds of many millions of Christians.

Now Tim LaHaye and Jerry Jenkins are interpreting this astonishing publishing phenomenon as an act of divine providence: this is the last opportunity for men and women to repent before the rapture occurs. God has ensured that their books sell well. And countless Christians are appreciating those books.

The Left Behind series should place the relative success of Dawkins, Harris, and Hitchens in context. The majority of people are still reading religious books; a small minority is starting to take an interest in atheism. Our atheist friends should not be misled: the truth is that they remain and will continue to remain a small minority worldview.

However, the fact that books by atheists are selling is significant. Earlier in the book, I suggested that the primary reason for this is our post-9/11 anxiety about Islam. It is also true that there are parts of the world that warm to their worldview. However, there is very little evidence that the secularization thesis is true.

The dominant trend: the secularization thesis

The secularization thesis is a hypothesis that links modernity with decreasing religious affiliation. Now, as Steve Bruce reminds us, there is no single "secularization thesis." However, Bruce writes, "The basic proposition is that modernization creates problems for religion."[5] So, to crudely oversimplify, as people become more affluent, more technologically able, and accept the remarkable narrative emerging from science, so religion decreases its hold over people. The main evidence for this has been the pattern of religious participation in Europe, where it is true that there has been a decline.

However, the problem for our atheist trio is that this is not true elsewhere in the world. The Muslim world remains as ardent as ever; in the United States, Gallup polls continue to demonstrate a committed 40 percent of the population is attending a religious congregation every week; and Christianity and Islam are both growing dramatically in Africa and other parts of the developing world. It almost looks as if Europe is the exception to the otherwise robustly religious trends in the rest of the world.

And even in Europe the data is puzzling. Grace Davie, who is probably one of the finest sociologists of religion working the UK today, points out that there are many contradictions embedded in the British (and European) experience. When Princess Diana died, churches were suddenly visited and everywhere countless flowers created "religious" shrines. In those countries with a Church tax, there are significant numbers who continue to pay it even though their practice is limited. So Grace Davie writes:

A crucial concept begins to emerge from these analyses: that of vicarious religion. Could it be that Europeans are not so much less religious than populations in other parts of the world, but – quite simply – differently so? For particular historical reasons (notably the historic connections between Church and State), significant numbers of Europeans are content to let both church and churchgoers enact a memory on their behalf (the essential meaning of vicarious), more than half way that they might need to draw on the capital at crucial times in their individual or their collective lives. The almost universal take up of religious ceremonies at the time of a death is the most obvious expression of this tendency; so, too, the prominence of the historic churches in particular times of national crisis or, more positively, of national celebration.[6]

Europeans are interesting: in Grace Davie's view, a minority is participating in religious practice on behalf of everyone else. By keeping these institutions going, this minority is ensuring that these institutions are available to everyone for certain rites of passage (especially death).

If Grace Davie is right and a religious minority is providing the religious witness on behalf of others, there is still a problem. The problem is that this minority is getting so small it is difficult to sustain these institutions. And this is not simply true of churches, but also of other organizations. If we compare Church participation with other organizations in civic society – such as the Rotary society, political parties, and Freemasons – we find that the decline in the Church is less than in these organizations.

If we focus for a moment on the UK, the British problem is that people do not want to join an organization. They don't mind going out to the pub or a movie, but they really don't want to run or organize a group around a shared interest or focus. Putnam's *Bowling Alone* has been realized. I suspect that the small minority who go to church are probably supporting other organizations. Nancy Ammerman in *Pillars of Faith* has demonstrated that Christians who participate in congregations are much more likely to be involved in other community organizations.[7]

Now this ought to worry Richard Dawkins. We are seeing in Britain the collapse of civic society. It is not unbelief that drives people away from the churches, but the power of the television and the demands of interacting with an organization. Dawkins ought to start "atheist societies" and certainly should be encouraging participation in the local amateur dramatic organization or a lobby group.

Journalists enjoy musing on whether the Church of England will exist in twenty years' time. The real question is whether any organizations will exist in twenty years' time. And, once society is at that point, there will be nothing for people to join. The church attendance statistics are worrying: but they ought to worry Richard Dawkins as well.

The persecuted minority

The other dynamic in these books is how atheists are persecuted. Dawkins provides several illustrations of the difficulties that atheists face. So it is true that you cannot be elected to public office in the United States if you are an atheist. In many respects, life can be difficult for the atheist.

Now, one significant human dynamic is that everyone likes to feel persecuted. So Rush Limbaugh, the very conservative talk-radio host, talks endlessly of a national liberal control of the "fly-by media" and the academy. He likes to feel persecuted. Meanwhile most liberals in America complain endlessly about the power of "oil interests," "health insurance companies," and "religious right," which control the conservatives in the Congress. The advantage of being persecuted is that one can turn one's cause into a moral crusade.

So it is important to remember this sense of being persecuted is partly a strategy that many different groups employ. However, let us concede that in some countries life can be difficult for the atheist. For example, in Saudi Arabia, it is difficult to be an atheist. Let us also concede that it can be difficult to get elected to office in the United States as an atheist, although it is interesting to see how African Americans, Hispanics, Muslims, and Jews have all been elected.

Ideally, we should all elect the best person for that position. So when an atheist is simply excluded because he or she is an atheist that is wrong. In the same way it would be wrong to make sexuality or race a decisive factor in an election. In many countries, especially European nations, being an atheist is not a problem for election to office. And, even in America, the atheist can keep the company of the comparably uncommitted and advocate for a strong secularism in public life. The American Civil Liberties Union has been a significant force in public life.

With the acknowledgment that prejudice over a single issue is always wrong, it must be observed that atheists have not been persecuted in the ways that, say, certain religious minorities faced. Atheists were not thrown to the lions by the Romans as were the Christians; atheists were not gassed in the Holocaust as were the Jews. And atheists have not had to cope with the struggles facing Christians under certain communist regimes.

Religion is part of the future. Atheists are an inevitable part of the pluralism of our future. They will form a small part. Ultimately, when it comes to important conversation partners, Muslims are always ahead of the atheists. However, all groups, regardless of their size, deserve the recognition of their fundamental human rights. And this obviously includes the atheists.

The Religious Future

Patterns of behavior will continue to vary. For some, a sense of spirituality, which does not express itself in any form of overt institutional participation, will be their religious life. For others, it will be more communal. The vast majority of people are continuing to believe – with good reason. God is continuing to get through. And there are plenty of forms of religion, the results of which will be dangerous, problematic, and strong.

Listening to the voice of the atheist can be helpful for the person of faith. It is often a challenging voice that makes us clarify what exactly we mean. Sometimes it is a call for social justice – are we really right to exclude this or that group from our sense of what makes a legitimate lifestyle? Persons of faith should listen and engage with the critique of the atheist. There is much of value that can be learned.

10

Faith and Uncertainty – Believing the Truth

So we come to the last chapter. One theme in this book has been the peculiar nature of knowing, with which humans are required to live. And, in this last chapter, we shall now return to this theme. A central claim is that underpinning the work of our atheist trio is the illusion of modernity. But the illusion is applied only to religion and never to science. This is a major inconsistency in their work.

One of their central targets is an unthinking "faith" – the faith that doesn't need reasons, yet is completely certain. Harris repeatedly takes aim at this target; he insists that this is what religious people really "mean" by faith. It is true that some religious people do use the word "faith" in a distinctively modern way. For some, it has become the refuge when all other explanations fail. So, for example, when the argument over evil and suffering gets tricky, we might hear someone say "well, it is all a matter of faith." When this happens, the religious person has also fallen captive to the illusion of modernity.

So what is this illusion? The illusion is this: modernity has connected knowledge with complete certainty and in so doing has found such knowledge is unobtainable. The net result is a reinterpretation of the word "faith" (to mean knowledge beyond reasons) or a relativism, or even a Nietzschian non-realism (i.e., all claims to knowledge are just human projections).

Now this is technical material, so let us unpack it more carefully. The philosopher Alasdair MacIntyre is most helpful here.

The problem begins with Descartes (1596–1650). He was a philosopher who argued that knowledge requires a certain foundation. Descartes in his discourses is reflecting on that central question of philosophy: how does he know? What can he be sure about? In the *Meditations of a First Philosophy* he starts by thinking about his knowledge of the external world. Is he sure that the external world exists? He decides he cannot be sure. He can never be sure that the external world exists; it is possible that the external world is a dream or – to use an image, which is available to us – we are all in the middle of the movie *The Matrix.*[1] So, for Descartes, we cannot be sure that what we see, touch, taste, or smell is really happening to us. Descartes then moves to mathematical truths. The problem here, explains Descartes, is the possibility of a malignant demon tampering with our brain cells, making us think that $2 + 2 = 4$. So now we are not even sure about mathematical truths. Just as an aside, this is an interesting moment in his argument because at this point he is in trouble. Once he postulates a malignant demon tampering with his brain cells to create mathematical assertions, he can no longer have any confidence that his logical powers of reasoning are working. So at that point he really should just stop writing. But he doesn't; he presses on. And he says, so what am I sure about? On what basis can I build my foundation of knowledge? He decides that the only foundation available to him is that very simple one – "I think therefore I am." Because I am doubting everything, there must be a me. This is the basis of knowledge.

Once we decide that knowledge requires complete certainty, our culture is in trouble. Certainly, metaphysics is in trouble: it is clear that complete certainty is unavailable to us. However, as the Scottish philosopher David Hume (1711–76) pointed out, it is not just a problem for metaphysics, but also for science. Science depends on uncertainty: science cannot prove – with certainty – the existence of the external world (it simply assumes its reality). It is from the Cartesian assumptions about knowledge that Nietzsche ends up with his view that "truth" is just projection.

Immanuel Kant (1724–1804) does attempt to provide a basis for science, while safeguarding religion. He distinguishes the world as it appears to the mind from the world of things as they are in themselves. In the former – the phenomenal world – Kant suggests that we can affirm science. Science appears to explain how the world appears to the mind. The mechanistic universe of Newton appears to explain the complexity of the world as it appears to the human mind. Kant also saw that religion was in trouble in this world. So, to save religion, Kant suggested that the world as it appears to the mind is different from the world of things as they are in themselves (the noumenal world). We know this latter world exists – after all, this world is responsible for our experiences. However, we don't know what this world is like because we cannot transcend our mind-interpreted world that we are constantly experiencing. However, it is possible that in this world religion might be true.

In a sense, Kant is responsible for the view that "faith" is a leap beyond what we know about this world and an act of non-rational trust that God is there. (In the *Critique of Practical Reason*, Kant is more complicated and explains that God is a necessary postulate of moral behavior.) However, as Nietzsche and others pointed out, Kant does not save either science or religion. Science is no longer "true" (in the sense of how the world really is) but is simply a mental interpretation of sense experience. I am sure that Dawkins wants to claim more than this. And religion remains unobtainable in a world that we don't even know exists.

The logic of the Cartesian (another way of talking about Descartes) assumption of knowledge is a Nietzschean projection. All truth has disappeared.

Alasdair MacIntyre's book *Whose Justice? Which Rationality?* argues that the Nietzschean destination is a result of an absurdity embedded in Descartes' assumption. This is an absurdity that no other age or tradition required. The absurdity was the expectation that all knowledge must be derived from an unquestionable certainty. To set this as the benchmark for knowledge makes knowledge impossible to obtain. As we have seen, the sciences cannot meet this expectation. We can always find reasons to question our senses – we might be dreaming or we may be in the middle of the film *The Matrix*. We can never be sure therefore, according to Enlightenment expectations for knowledge, that we have any knowledge. The mistake, MacIntyre explains, is to set this absurd expectation for knowledge. Instead of requiring conceptual certainty, we need to recognize the tradition-constituted nature of all knowledge. We are not able to transcend our rootedness. We are not able to get outside our minds and bodies and view the world from some Archimedean viewpoint. Instead, we are all living inside a tradition. And the purpose of the traditions that we all occupy (be it secular, Catholic, Protestant, Sunni, or whatever) is to make sense of the complexity of the world. And we compare different traditions by learning to live inside two simultaneously, and by comparing the result in terms of explanatory power and coherence. As we do so, we can then decide between traditions.

Being Located

So we return to a theme of this book. We are made in place. Learning is difficult. It is a complex process of data, interpretation, language, and contextualization. It happens gradually. It involves training; if you sit with someone who really appreciates fine wine, then you can learn to associate certain words with distinctive smells and tastes. And what is true of wine is true of sport, science, and religion.

Theologically, it is clear that God always intended humanity to learn through struggle. Although conceptually one can imagine a different universe, in this one the learning process takes time. It starts in families, extends through communities, and involves learning languages. It involves both beliefs and practices.

There are certain virtues that are cultivated through this sort of process. All learning involves community – learning cannot happen in isolation. Humility is forced on us: we are not allowed to have everything sorted. Our worldview always needs an element of openness and must be revisable. Someone who takes our epistemological situation seriously will have to recognize that we are always seeing through "a glass darkly" (1 Corinthians: 13).

Faith and Trust

Faith is grounded on reasons, open to the possibility of revision, and an act of trust in God. *Contra* Sam Harris, this is simply a description of the classical view of faith. Aquinas, the hero of Roman Catholic theology, would concur. He insisted on the centrality of arguments as a foundation for faith; he believed that God-given reason should be able to establish the nature and existence of God. He was always willing to engage with the finest non-Christian thought to shape his theology. And, although he believed he was offering the strongest account of the Christian faith available in his age, he knew that it was a significant modification on the Augustinian system that had shaped his intellectual formation.

So, as with all worldviews that seek to be compelling, it is essential that there is a rich conversation with good arguments and reasons. One should seek to ensure that one's account of the transcendent is internally coherent and that the evidence available for faith is clearly described. In this book, I have identified a variety of pointers that suggest the plausibility of the God hypothesis. None of these arguments are decisive individually, but taken together they are compelling.

In fact all arguments in all subjects have a similar character. Descartes' quest for a certain foundation on which all knowledge can be built has failed. Even in science, we have a much more fluid picture of models engaging with data and the model, and then being modified. So, with faith, we offer an account that seems to make sense of our experience and builds on the insights embedded in our tradition, which will in time be modified and amended. God does not want us to have a single description that will be timelessly true. However, this does not mean our descriptions are just projections, which cannot be ranked as stronger or weaker. Instead, we use the traditional criteria – coherence and explanatory power – and judge the descriptions by those criteria.

Reason, then, is an essential part of faith. When we talk about humanity being made in the "Image of God," we are talking (among other things) about the human capacity to think and reason. Any account of faith that does not stress the importance of reasons denies the doctrine of the *Imago Dei* (the Image of God). God intended us to use the faculty of reason as part of the process of discerning a truer account of the transcendent.

Given the importance of reason, faith also must be revisable. One of the frustrations with our three atheists is their lack of sense that the tradition is constantly struggling to discern the truth about God. And, on the way, there have been countless mistakes. Religion was mistaken to sacrifice children to appease the divine; religion was wrong to sanction patriarchy and slavery; and religion was wrong to advocate genocide.

We are living at a time when we are finally recognizing that religion needs to accommodate the scientific insight of homosexual orientation. The author of Leviticus and St Paul in Romans did not know about homosexual orientation. Leviticus wants the Hebrews to live differently from their neighbors (an obligation that continues to be binding on all of God's people in all cultures); the extraordinary Genesis story of Lot in Sodom is clearly prohibiting gang rape of men (a prohibition I continue to affirm); and Paul has a vice-list (to use the technical term) in Romans that condemns experimental homosexual sex. None of these texts are condemning two men or two women who are committed and faithful to each other. So, for these reasons, many Christians (myself included) are arguing that the biblical Christian should affirm same-sex marriage.

Harris and Dawkins are aware of "liberal" Christians, who in their view are no longer Christians. Now it is true that there are some Christians who are very cavalier about our sources, and imaginative in the ways that they are conceiving the Christian story (John Shelby Spong is a good illustration of this). However, the majority of Anglicans and their counterparts in other denominations are simply doing the work that our predecessors did on other social issues in their day. The tradition has always been open. We still believe that the Eternal Word is disclosed in the life, death, and resurrection of Jesus. We are still trying to read that life accurately and seeking to understand what God requires of us. We are still properly and theologically conservative. And, as an act of faithfulness to our tradition, we are suggesting how it might revisit a traditional prohibition on all same-sex intimacy and recognize that it was never intended that monogamous same-sex relationships should be forbidden.

But am I sure?

Richard Dawkins is "sure" that there is not a God. In this respect it is appropriate to describe him and his fellow travelers as "fundamentalist atheists." As with the Christian authors of the *The Fundamentals,* there is no room for ambiguity or humility or nuance. This chapter has argued that our human condition does not allow us such certainty. The Creeds start with "I believe." Even when it is grounded in reason, faith is still an act of assertion. In effect, the Creeds invite us to believe that Christianity is true.

"I believe that Christianity is true." The first part of this sentence, "I believe," does recognize our human condition. It does recognize the fact that certainty is not permitted. As we have seen, if there is one lesson that we should have learned from modernity, then that is the fact (about which we can be certain perhaps) that certainty will always evade us. We are all in the business of making assumptions that we cannot prove (for example, the existence of the external world and that we are not all figments of a person's imagination); we are all constructing models and constantly exploring their plausibility, coherence, and explanatory power. This is the way the world is. This is the way that God has made this world.

The "I believe" also recognizes the inevitable pluralism of views that this epistemological reality creates for us. When it comes to economics, history, and science, disagreement is inevitable. Agreement in most disciplines is difficult to reach. So we have to live with a diversity of views.

It is partly because this is the way that God made creation that I am confident God will be merciful to those who opt for a different metaphysical interpretation of the world. There are plenty of reasons, embedded in Scripture, for us to expect that heaven will include Muslims, Buddhists, Jews, Hindus, and Christians. The God of Scripture is a God of surprises. In fact, I am expecting to encounter a redeemed Richard Dawkins, Christopher Hitchens, and Sam Harris. After all, as Jesus put it to Nicodemus, the "spirit blows where it wills" (John 3).

The "I believe" captures all that must be provisional in our worldview. It captures an inevitable provisionality that God has built into the creation. However, the last part of the sentence is the affirmation of faith. As a person who is seeking the truth about God and God's relationship to the world, I believe that a strand of the Christian community has it right. And by "right" I mean it is truer than the current alternative worldviews available. In the same way as we hold political views (about Iraq or global warming), we all take positions trusting that these – insofar as we can judge – are right (or at least more right than the alternatives). Metaphysical positions are in principle no different. It is important to stress the "strand of the Christian community"; it is not that all Christians are right and all Muslims are wrong. That would be a silly thing to say: after all, there is a lot of overlap between Christians and Muslims, and certain strands of Islam and certain strands of Christianity have more in common with each other than those strands have with other strands in the same religion. So the strand that I believe to be more right than the alternatives is the Anglican tradition, with a Catholic shaping, which is Trinitarian, Incarnational, and Eucharistic-centered.

So, in summary, the "I believe" part recognizes that my ecumenical and interfaith friends see things differently, and that difference in the world is divinely intended. The "Christianity is true" part of the statement captures my conviction that a certain strand of Christianity is coherent, plausible, and explains the complexity of the data. The question "Am I completely sure?" is one that I refuse to answer. It accepts a standard for knowing that is absurd. I am not "completely sure" that I am not dreaming; so what could it mean to be completely sure about metaphysics? We need to learn to live with divinely intended pluralism, which runs parallel with the affirmation all of us should make – an affirmation that a particular understanding of the world makes more sense than the alternatives. Accepting pluralism and affirming truth should not be seen as positions that are opposites or incompatible.

Conclusion

What would Natalie want to say to Fred? She would want to explain that faith is not like a belief in Santa Claus. Instead, it is a serious interpretation of the world that makes sense of the complexity of the data. She would want to stress that much of science points to the truth of theism. But, most important of all, she would want to help Fred see that there are countless moments when he is on the cusp of "seeing" – those moments when he is in love, or enjoying great music, or getting angry about injustice.

Atheism is not a silly worldview. At certain points in many lives, doubt may arise as we struggle with particular questions. The opening chapter was an important exercise: we need to recognize that there is a challenge embedded in these books, even if the challenge has not always been posed as well as it could have been. And I am grateful to this trinity of atheists who have afforded me with an opportunity to provide a response. The response has had six aspects.

The first is the identification of a "spiritual sense" that enables us to see the transcendent in everything around us. The various pointers for faith (the nature of love, the fact of beauty, and our deep moral intuitions) are really all part of our "spiritual sense." The reason why it is important to introduce faith to children (and an act of child cruelty not to do so) is that it is in childhood that the gift of faith is discovered – the spiritual sense is nurtured. In the same way that children can absorb many languages, learn to appreciate music, and cultivate a capacity through taste to enjoy a range of foods, so children have a capacity to see and appreciate the divine. And in the same way, just as learning a language is difficult for an adult, so it can be difficult for an adult to see the spiritual side of the world.

The second is the theme of locatedness and rootedness. Sociology is an important discipline because it concentrates on this phenomenon. Knowing is always local. It is always difficult. Almost everything is complicated. It seems as if God set the world up in such a way that we would always be in the business of truth-seeking and holding those truths with humility. Persons of faith, as they reflect on this fact about creation, should be committed to pluralism and conversation.

The third theme is that science is now one of the best reasons for faith. And interestingly there are plenty of scientists who would affirm that judgment. Richard Dawkins suggests that most scientists are skeptics, but Francis Collins points out:

> And what about spiritual belief amongst scientists? This is actually more prevalent than many realize. In 1916, researchers asked biologists, physicists, and mathematicians whether they believed in God, who actively communicates with humankind and to whom one may pray in expectation of receiving an answer. About 40 percent answered in the affirmative. In 1997, the same survey was repeated verbatim – and to the surprise of the researchers, the percentage remained very nearly the same.[1]

In particular, physics is in a very different place from biology. Whereas biology is preoccupied with its recent discoveries and how best to explain them, physics is coping with the remarkable math underpinning this universe and the murky world at the quantum level. Both of these areas are important for theism. The math of the universe is a good argument for faith; and the discoveries at the quantum level are providing an insight into how God might be acting in the world.

The fourth theme is that these books are emerging now because of Islamaphobia. Our atheists constantly complain that religion feeds hatred and intolerance, without noticing that their

books are feeding hatred and intolerance of Islam. It is important for anyone interested in the world today to work hard to
understand the dynamics within Islam. And it is important to know
that the majority of Muslims do not live in the Middle East;
everyone should be aware of the internal diversity of Islam – from
versions of Islam deeply committed to non-violence to those
willing to contemplate *jihad* against the West. Leaving aside Sam
Harris's enthusiasm for torture, he has written a book that adds
to the misunderstanding and fear of Islam.

And the final theme is that the atheism of Dawkins, Hitchens,
and Harris is not facing up to its own implications. They need to
read their co-atheist Nietzsche more closely. Our atheist trio wants
to advocate an atheism that doesn't really challenge anything.
However, the implications of their worldview are much more
challenging. Nietzsche suspects that the language of morality does
not make any sense once the God-symbol goes; and Nietzsche
suspects that the assumptions underpinning science are ultimately theistic.

The argument of this book is that Nietzsche is right: the implications of atheism are much more dramatic than the Oxbridge
atheism being advocated by Dawkins. The real choice is much
more dramatic than Dawkins would lead a person to believe. Moral
language becomes meaningless; science is no more than a linguistic activity that seems to work for a small locality. Perhaps
the fact that neither Dawkins nor Hitchens can even go there is
more evidence for the truth of theism.

Notes

Chapter 1 Getting inside Fundamentalist Atheism: The Gentle Atheism of Dawkins, Hitchens, and Harris

1 See Richard Dawkins, *The God Delusion* (London: Transworld Publishers Black Swan, 2006), p. 319f.

2 Sam Harris has a soft spot for certain forms of Eastern religion. But he shares his fellow atheists' commitments to the destructive nature of the Abrahamic traditions.

3 Perhaps in a note I should clarify my precise ecclesial home. I am an Episcopal priest and trained in the Anglican tradition. The strongest strand of Anglicanism is the Anglo-Catholic tradition. The hero of my *Truth and the Reality of God* (Edinburgh: T. & T. Clark, 1998) was Aquinas; the hero of my *Theology of Engagement* (Oxford: Blackwell, 2003) was Augustine.

4 See St. Thomas Aquinas, *Summa Theologica*, various translators (London: Blackfriars, various dates).

5 It did not get as fair as formal censure, although the Archbishop of Canterbury did issue a list of propositions, many of which were linked with Aquinas. This episode is described at the start of Brian Davies's excellent introduction to *The Thought of Thomas Aquinas* (Oxford: Oxford University Press, 1992).

6 See Christopher Hitchens, *God is Not Great: How Religion Poisons Everything* (New York and Boston: Twelve Hachette Book Group, 2007).

7 Sam Harris, *The End of Faith: Religion, Terror and the Future of Reason* (New York and London: W. W. Norton, 2004).

8   Sam Harris, *The End of Faith*, pp. 57–8.
9   I am aware that those sympathetic to astrology would disagree with the inclusion of the word "entirely" as part of their beliefs.
10 Richard Dawkins, *The God Delusion*, p. 52.
11 Ibid., p. 59.
12 Sam Harris, *The End of Faith*, p. 173.
13 Richard Dawkins, *The God Delusion*, p. 55.
14 Sam Harris, *The End of Faith*, p. 65.
15 Bertrand Russell, as quoted by Richard Dawkins, *The God Delusion*, p. 75.
16 Richard Dawkins, *The God Delusion*, p. 77.
17 John Hick, *Philosophy of Religion* (Englewood Cliffs, NJ: Prentice-Hall, 1963), p. 30.
18 Richard Dawkins, *The God Delusion*, p. 52; his italics.
19 Thomas Crean, OP, makes this point in *God is No Delusion: A Refutation of Richard Dawkins* (San Francisco: Ignatius Press, 2007), p. 11.
20 See Edward Harrison, "The Natural Selection of Universes Containing Intelligent Life," in *Quarterly Journal of the Royal Astronomical Society*, 36: 193–203.
21 It is perhaps helpful to note that this does not require Dawkins to disprove Russell's "teapot." Materialism is a positive philosophical claim about the nature of reality: if it is true, then Dawkins needs arguments to establish its truth.
22 Richard Dawkins, *The God Delusion*, p. 178.
23 Thomas Crean, *God is No Delusion*, p. 15.
24 Ibid., p. 28.
25 Christopher Hitchens, *God is Not Great*, p. 64.
26 Ibid., p. 85.
27 Ibid., p. 88.
28 Sam Harris, *The End of Faith*, p. 48.
29 Ibid., p. 92.
30 Richard Dawkins, *The God Delusion*, p. 327.
31 Ibid., p. 300.
32 Ibid., p. 251.
33 Christopher Hitchens, *God is Not Great*, p. 283.
34 Sam Harris, *The End of Faith*, pp. 109–10.
35 Richard Dawkins, *The God Delusion*, p. 51.
36 Ibid., pp. 347–8.
37 Christopher Hitchens, *God is Not Great*, p. 217.
38 Richard Dawkins, *The God Delusion*, p. 381.
39 Christopher Hitchens, *God is Not Great*, p. 41.

40 Ibid., pp. 38–9.
41 Ibid., p. 39.
42 Ibid., p. 40.
43 Jacob Milgrom, *Leviticus 1–16: A New Translation with Introduction and Commentary* (New York: Doubleday, 1991), p. 735.
44 Christopher Hitchens, *God is Not Great*, p. 41.
45 Jacob Milgrom, *Leviticus 1–16*, p. 652.

Chapter 2 Nietzsche: The Last Real Atheist

1 I have discussed the work of Nietzsche in two other places. The implications of Nietzsche for the concept of truth is developed in my *Truth and Reality of God* (Edinburgh: T. & T. Clark, 1999), chapter 6, and the implications of Nietzsche for ethics is developed in *Do Morals Matter?* (Oxford: Blackwell, 2007). Some of the material that follows is dependent on these earlier discussions.
2 See Walter Kaufmann, *Nietzsche: Philosopher, Psychologist, Antichrist*, 4th edn (Princeton: Princeton University Press, 1974).
3 F. Nietzsche, *Beyond Good and Evil*, translated by R. J. Hollingdale, introduction by Michael Tanner (Harmondsworth: Penguin, 1990), section 14, p. 44.
4 F. Nietzsche, *Ecce Homo*, translated by R. J. Hollingdale, introduction by M. Tanner (Harmondsworth: Penguin, 1992), p. 44.
5 Ibid., p. 18. Nietzsche writes, "I perceive physiologically – smell – the proximity or . . . the innermost parts, the 'entrails,' of every soul."
6 Gary Shapiro, "Friedrich Nietzsche," in Chad Meister and Paul Copan (eds.), *The Routledge Companion to Philosophy of Religion* (Oxford and New York: Routledge, 2007), p. 171.
7 The correspondence theory of truth is the view that a proposition is true when it corresponds to the way things are in reality.
8 "On Truth and Lies in a Nonmoral Sense," in *Philosophy and Truth*, translated and edited by Daniel Breazeale (New Jersey: Humanities Press, 1979), p. 79.
9 Ibid., p. 80; my italics.
10 Ibid., p. 82.
11 Ibid., p. 84.
12 Ibid., p. 85.
13 F. Nietzsche, *Human, All Too Human*, translated by R. J. Hollingdale, introduction by Richard Schacht (Cambridge: Cambridge University Press, 1996), p. 12.

14   Ibid., p. 12.
15   Ibid., p. 13.
16   F. Nietzsche, *The Gay Science*, translated with commentary by Walter Kaufmann (New York: Vintage Books, 1974), book two, section 57, p. 121.
17   Ibid., book two, section 57, p. 121.
18   Ibid., book two, section 58, pp. 121–2.
19   F. Nietzsche, *Beyond Good and Evil*, translated by R. J. Hollingdale, introduction by M. Tanner (Harmondsworth: Penguin, 1990), section 17, p. 47.
20   Ibid., section 23, pp. 53–4.
21   F. Nietzsche, *The Gay Science*, translated with commentary by Walter Kaufmann (New York: Vintage Books, 1974), book five, section 111, p. 172.
22   R. J. Hollingdale, in F. Nietzsche, *Thus Spake Zarathustra*, translated with an introduction by R. J. Hollingdale (Harmondsworth: Penguin, 1969), pp. 25–6.
23   F. Nietzsche, *Thus Spake Zarathustra*, translated with an introduction by R. J. Hollingdale (Harmondsworth: Penguin, 1969), part one, section 3, p. 43.
24   Ibid., part one, section 3, p. 43.
25   Ibid., part one, section 3, p. 42.
26   Ibid., part one, section 3, p. 103. Nietzsche is very proud of this exhortation from Zarathustra. He quotes it at length in *Ecce Homo*; perhaps a comment on all of Nietzsche's teaching. See F. Nietzsche, *Ecce Homo*, translated by R. J. Hollingdale, introduction by M. Tanner (Harmondsworth: Penguin, 1992), pp. 5–6.
27   F. Nietzsche, *Twilight of the Idols*, translated by Richard Polt, introduction by Tracy Strong (Indianapolis: Hackett Publishing, 1997), pp. 23–4.

Chapter 3   Appreciating the Faith Discourse

1   Jared Diamond, *Guns, Germs, and Steel: The Fates of Human Societies* (New York and London: W. W. Norton, 1999), p. 256.
2   Steven Pinker and Ray Jackendoff, "The Faculty of Language: What's Special about It," in *Cognition*, 95 (2005): 224. Chomsky's views have changed across his corpus: the particular paper that Pinker and Jackendoff are challenging is found in M. D. Hauser, N. Chomsky, and W. T. Fitch, "The Faculty of Language: What it is, Who Has it, and How Did it Evolve?," in *Science*, 298: 1569–79.

3   Parts of this section are taken from my *Understanding Christian Doctrine* (Oxford: Blackwell, 2008).

4   David Hay, *Something There: The Biology of the Human Spirit* (West Conshohocken, PA: Templeton Foundation Press, 2006), p. xi.

5   Ibid., p. 11.

6   Ibid., p. 9.

7   Ibid., p. 37.

8   This discussion of religious experience draws on my discussion in *Understanding Christian Doctrine* (Oxford: Blackwell, 2008).

9   Richard Swinburne, *The Existence of God* (Oxford: Clarendon Press, 1979), p. 254.

10 Ibid., p. 272.

11 Some of the discussion that follows draws heavily on my *Understanding Christian Doctrine* (Oxford: Blackwell, 2008).

12 I am assuming that only adults are reading this book. If you are child, then I do apologize for suggesting that Santa Claus might not exist. Of course, it is possible that Santa does exist; the spirit of Christmas is real enough.

13 George Steiner, *Real Presences* (Chicago, IL: University of Chicago Press, 1989), p. 3.

14 Ibid., p. 182.

15 Ibid., p. 191.

16 Ibid., p. 201.

17 Ibid., p. 228.

18 Ibid., p. 215.

Chapter 4   Physics: The Grown-up Science

1   Pierre-Simon Laplace, *A Philosophical Essay on Probablities*, translated by Frederick Truscott and Frederick Emory (London: Chapman and Hall, 1902), p. 4.

2   Keith Ward, *Divine Action* (London: Collins Flame, 1990), p. 83.

3   Keith Ward, *The Battle for the Soul* (London: Hodder and Stoughton, 1985), pp. 47–8.

4   Keith Ward, *Divine Action*, p. 59.

5   Paul Davies, *Cosmic Jackpot: Why Our universe is Just Right for Life* (New York: Orion Productions, 2007), p. 150.

6   Ibid., p. 150.

7   Paul Davies, *God and the New Physics* (London: Penguin, 1983), p. 179.

8   Ibid., p. 181.
9   See J. D. Barrow and F. J. Tipler, *The Anthropic Cosmological Principle* (Oxford: Oxford University Press, 1986).
10   See M. J. Rees, *Just Six Numbers: The Deep Forces that Shape the Universe* (London: Weidenfeld & Nicolson, 1999).
11   See Stephen Hawking, *The Universe in a Nutshell* (London: Bantam, 2001).
12   See Rodney D. Holder, *God, the Multiverse, and Everything* (Aldershot: Ashgate, 2004).
13   Richard Dawkins, *The God Delusion*, p. 171.
14   Ibid., p. 171.
15   Ibid., p. 165.
16   Paul Davies, *Cosmic Jackpot*, p. 173.
17   Richard Dawkins, *The God Delusion*, p. 188.
18   Rodney Holder, *God, the Multiverse, and Everything* (Aldershot: Ashgate, 2004), p. 123.
19   Ibid., pp. 123–4.
20   Paul Badham, "Reflections on the Craig–Flew Debate," in *Modern Believing*, July 2008, 49 (3): 26–7.
21   Stan W. Wallace (ed.), *Does God Exist? The Craig–Flew Debate* (Aldershot: Ashgate, 2003), p. 24.
22   Ibid., p. 26.
23   Anthony Flew, *There is a God. How the World's Most Notorious Atheist Changed His Mind* (New York: HarperCollins, 2007), pp. 113–14.
24   Ibid., pp. 119–21.

Chapter 5   A Revealing God

1   As quoted by Dan Brown, in the *DaVinci Code* by the character Teabing.
2   John Mbiti, *African Religion and Philosophy* (Garden City: Doubleday Publishing, 1970), p. 56.
3   John Mbiti, *Concepts of God in Africa* (New York: Praeger Publishers, 1970), p. 8.
4   Arthur Peacocke, *Theology for a Scientific Age* (London: SCM Press, 1993), enlarged edn, p. 56.
5   Anne Primavesi, *From Apocalypse to Genesis* (Kent: Burns and Oates, 1991), p. 234.
6   Ibid., p. 43.
7   Richard Dawkins, *The God Delusion*, p. 280.
8   Ibid., p. 280.

Chapter 6 Christianity

1 Christopher Hitchens, *God is Not Great*, p. 120. Richard Dawkins is also an admirer of Bart Ehrman. See Richard Dawkins, *The God Delusion*, pp. 120–1.

2 Much like both Hitchens and Dawkins, I have also spent significant time with the writings of Bart Ehrman. For a fuller discussion of his views, see my *Understanding Christian Doctrine* (Oxford: Blackwell, 2008). This summary of Ehrman draws, in places, on this fuller discussion.

3 Bart D. Ehrman, *Jesus: Apocalyptic Prophet of the New Millennium* (Oxford: Oxford University Press, 1999), p. 3.

4 Ibid., p. 119.

5 Ibid., p. 148.

6 Ibid., p. 150.

7 Ibid., p. 158.

8 Ibid., p. 161.

9 Ibid., p. 217.

10 Larry W. Hurtado, *Lord Jesus Christ*, p. 650.

11 Karl Barth, *Church Dogmatics*, Volume 1, Part 2 (Edinburgh: T. & T. Clark, 1963), p. 513.

12 Ibid., pp. 530–1.

13 I do, of course, recognize that reading the Qur'an is difficult. And I am very interested in the various ways in which the Qur'an is interpreted, particularly with the emphasis on those verses that have local significance and those that have more universal significance.

14 Richard Dawkin, *The God Delusion*, p. 15.

15 Mike Higton, "Undoing Delusion," in *Conversations in Religion and Theology*, 6 (1), May 2008: 4.

16 Ibid., p. 5.

Chapter 7 Islam

1 Tina Beattie, *The New Atheists: The Twilight of Reason and the War on Religion* (London: Darton Longman and Todd, 2007), pp. 87–90.

2 Sam Harris, *The End of Faith*, pp. 117–23. To his credit, Harris does admit that "this is all desperately tedious."

3 Eric Cantana is the French soccer player who played for Manchester United and became known as the soccer philosopher.

4   Some of this material is taken from Ian Markham with Christy Lohr, *A World Religions Reader*, 3rd edn (Oxford: Wiley-Blackwell, 2009). See this volume for a fuller description of Islam.

5   11. The Five Pillars. Hadith. Bukhari, *The Book of Belief (i.e. Faith)* No. 7. (Muhammad Muhsin Khan, *The Translation of the Meanings of Sahih Al-Bukhari* (Chicago, IL: Kazi Publications, 1976), p. 17.

6   Islam is very varied; there are other groups that are committed to both peace, dialogue, and pluralism. Almost any strand of Islam that is significantly influenced by "Sufism" is in this group, which perhaps makes up the majority of Muslims.

7   Lindsey O'Rourke, "Behind the Woman Behind the Bomb," in *The New York Times*, August 2, 2008, p. A27.

8   Ibid.

9   Greg Barton, *Jemaah Islamiyah: Radical Islamism in Indonesia* (Singapore: Ridge Books, 2005), see especially chapter 2.

10   I am grateful to Max Farrer, who makes this point in his thoughtful description of the impulses behind the London bombers. See Max Farrer, in "When Alienation Turns to Nihilism: The Dilemmas Posed for Diversity Post 7/7," *Conversations in Religion and Theology*, 4 (1): 98–123.

11   Seyyid Qutb, *Milestones* (Damascus, Syria: Dar al-ilm, no date), p. 27.

12   Ibid., pp. 30–1.

13   Ibid., p. 48.

14   Ibid., p. 62.

15   Greg Barton, *Jemaah Islamiyah*, p. 41.

16   Greg Barton, *Jemaah Islamiyah*, p. 41.

Chapter 8   Suffering, Providence, and Horrid Religious People

1   Keith Ward, *Divine Action* (London: Collins Flame, 1990), p. 48.

2   Ibid.

3   Keith Ward, *Divine Action*, p. 126. The quotation inside is from Prigogene and Stengers.

4   Keith Ward, *Divine Action*, p. 166.

5   Ibid., p. 159.

6   Richard Dawkins, *The God Delusion*, p. 285.

7   Borden Painter, "The New Atheism: Denying God and History," in *Conversations in Religion and Theology*, 6 (1), May 2008: 93.

Chapter 9   Religion and the Future

1   Richard Dawkins, *The God Delusion*, p. 13.
2   Ibid., p. 380. The idea here is that in the same way advocates for the homosexual lifestyle successfully coopted the word "gay," so atheists should coopt the word "brights."
3   See Beverly Rykerd, "Left Behind Series Sells 50 Millionth Copy," on: <www.leftbehind.com/channelnews>.
4   Ibid.
5   Steve Bruce, *God is Dead: Secularization in the West* (Oxford: Blackwell, 2002), p. 2.
6   Grace Davie, *Europe: The Exceptional Case* (London: Darton Longman and Todd, 2002), p. 19.
7   Nancy Ammerman, *Pillars of Faith: American Congregations and Their Partners* (Berkeley/Los Angeles/London: University of California Press, 2005).

Chapter 10   Faith and Uncertainty – Believing the Truth

1   The film *Matrix* describes a world where we are enjoying computer-generated experiences while lying in a vast bathtub.

Conclusion

1   Francis S. Collins, *The Language of God: A Scientist Presents Evidence for Belief* (New York: Free Press, 2006), p. 4.

Select Bibliography

Many major themes have been introduced in this short book. So, for those who want to explore these questions in more detail, the following books are worth studying.

On the Science

Paul Davies, *God and the New Physics* (London: Penguin, 1983).
Anything by Paul Davies is worth reading. And several of his books are listed in this section. A truly great book, which does not simply describe the anthropic principle, but also explains the mysteries of the physics at the quantum level.

Paul Davies, *The Fifth Miracle: The Search for the Origin and Meaning of Life*
    (New York, London, Sydney, Singapore: Simon & Schuster, 1999).
In this book, he deals with the factors that generate life and touches on a range of related issues, for example, the possibility of life on other planets.

Paul Davies, *Cosmic Jackpot: Why Our Universe is Just Right for Life* (Boston
    and New York: Houghton Mifflin Co., 2007).
A good summary of the growing data of evidence that indicates just how incredible the math is that produced a bio-friendly universe.

Rodney D. Holder, *God, the Multiverse, and Everything: Modern Cosmology
    and the Argument from Design* (Aldershot: Ashgate, 2004).

A very competent philosopher looks at the issues and debates around the multiverse hypothesis and shows that the arguments for the alternative are flawed.

On Atheism

Stan W. Wallace, *Does God Exist? The Craig–Flew Debate* (Aldershot: Ashgate, 2003).
A good summary of the debate between Craig and Flew. Craig is the theist; and Flew is the atheist.

Anthony Flew with Roy Abraham Varghese, *There is a God: How the World's Most Notorious Atheist Changed His Mind* (New York: HarperOne, 2007).
It is a pity that the book is not more substantial, but it does tell the story of how Anthony Flew changed his mind on the question of God.

Tina Beattie, *The New Atheists: The Twilight of Reason and the War on Religion* (London: Darton Longman and Todd, 2007).
A postmodern look at the narratives underpinning science. Beattie argues that the scientific conceit of Dawkins et al. is indicative of a crisis within our world.

Thomas Crean, OP, *God is No Delusion: A Refutation of Richard Dawkins* (San Francisco: Ignatius Press, 2007).
With some care, Thomas Crean exposes the philosophical confusions underpinning much of Dawkins's arguments. Less good on the theology and Bible, but outstanding on the arguments.

On Theology

Ian Markham, *Understanding Christian Doctrine* (Oxford: Blackwell, 2008).
For the person interested in what Christians are trying to say when they use words like "trinity" and "incarnation," this book is for them.

Keith Ward, *The Battle for the Soul* (London: Hodder and Stoughton, 1985).
A good solid discussion of the challenges facing personhood in modernity. Ward makes the case for the soul and attacks the reductionism pervading so much modern science.

The Fundamentals booklet series (1910–15), articulating commitments to the inerrancy of Scripture, a substitutionary atonement, and a literal return of Jesus to Earth, is reproduced on a website: <http://www. geocities.com/Athens/Parthenon/6528/fundcont.htm>.

On Providence and Prayer

Keith Ward, *Divine Action* (London: Collins Flame, 1990).
This is an exceptionally good book that makes the case that the world-view emerging from the New Physics opens up an account of divine providence, which is plausible, powerful, and faithful.

Philip Clements-Jewery, *Intercessory Prayer: Modern Theology, Biblical Teaching and Philosophical Thought* (Aldershot: Ashgate, 2005).
A good survey of the biblical and theological themes around this important topic.

On Sociology

Grace Davie, *Europe: The Exceptional Case* (London: Darton Longman and Todd, 2002).
A good accessible summary of her major works (*Religion in Modern Europe: A Memory Mutates*). It provides a global survey of religion throughout the world and explains that Europe is less religious than it appears.

Index